Goose Patch Co. ®

A Country Store In Your Mailbox®

Family Favorites

A cozy keepsake
of recipes & memories,
golden moments &
treasured traditions
from our family to yours.

A Country Store In Your Mailbox®

Gooseberry Patch
149 Johnson Drive
Department BOOK
Delaware, OH 43015
★
1·800·85·GOOSE
1-800·854·6673

Copyright 1997, Gooseberry Patch® 1-888052-21-X
Third Printing, May, 1999

How To Subscribe

Would you like to receive
"A Country Store in Your Mailbox"®?
For a 2-year subscription to our 88-page
Gooseberry Patch catalog, simply send $3.00 to:

Gooseberry Patch
149 Johnson Drive
Department BOOK
Delaware, OH 43015

Contents

DEDICATION

To families everywhere
whose traditions of today
make the memories of tomorrow.

APPRECIATION

To everyone in our Gooseberry Patch family
who has shared a warm thought,
a memorable moment or a
favorite recipe, we thank you!

Rise & Shine

☆ Take time for breakfast! ☆

Papa's Potato Pancakes

Mrs. Donald Messer
Beloit, WI

This recipe is my favorite because Papa made them with love when we were children. I remember it because my mother died when I was ten years old and my father was both mother and father to my brother, sister and me. He taught me to cook and the importance of good ingredients. His potato pancakes were a special treat since we didn't have them every day. My father always served them with grilled sausage and applesauce. There was a shaker of cinnamon and one of nutmeg on the table to add to the applesauce. Sometimes we really made a mess in the kitchen, but always had a room full of love.

4 to 6 medium potatoes,
    enough to make 3 cups
    grated
1 small onion
2 eggs

3 T. flour
1 t. salt
1/4 t. baking powder
1/4 c. milk

Grate potatoes and onion, add eggs mixing well. In another bowl combine flour, salt and baking powder. Combine with potato mixture, adding milk. Pour small amounts onto a lightly oiled hot griddle. Fry until golden on both sides. Makes 16 medium-size pancakes.

Papa's Apple Sauce

Make bacon curls to garnish your breakfast plate. Fry bacon until browned but not crisp; immediately roll up slices and fasten each with a toothpick. Drain on paper towels.

Sour Cream Coffee Cake

Lois Mahoney
Casper, WY

This coffee cake recipe was handed down by my grandmother from Maryland. When I was 14 years old and in 4-H, my mother suggested it for my cooking project entry at the fair. It won the First Prize at the county fair! The pride was shared by my mother, grandmother and of course, myself!

1/2 c. butter
1/2 c. shortening
1-1/4 c. sugar
2 eggs, beaten
1 c. sour cream

1 t. vanilla
1/2 t. baking soda
2 c. cake flour
1 t. baking powder

Cream butter, shortening and sugar. Add eggs, sour cream and vanilla. Beat well and gradually add sifted dry ingredients. Mix well. Pour half the batter in a buttered 9-inch tube pan. Sprinkle with half the topping mixture.

Topping:

1/2 c. walnuts, finely
   chopped
2 T. sugar

1/2 t. cinnamon
1/8 t. nutmeg

Combine topping ingredients and sprinkle half over coffee cake batter. Add remaining batter and remaining topping mix. Bake at 350 degrees for one hour.

Sweet Potato Muffins

Faye Hood
Newport News, VA

This recipe has been passed down for three generations.

1/2 c. butter
1-1/4 c. sugar
2 eggs
1-1/4 c. mashed sweet
    potatoes
1-1/2 c. self-rising flour
3 t. baking powder
1/4 t. salt

1/8 t. baking soda
1 t. cinnamon
1/4 t. nutmeg
1/4 t. allspice
1 c. milk
1/4 c. walnuts
1/4 c. raisins

Combine all ingredients and bake at 400 degrees in greased muffin tins for 25 minutes.

Seek home for rest, for home is best.

- Proverb

Griddle Cakes

Tami Bowman
Gooseberry Patch

My great-grandma Nora's recipe has been in the Nicol family for four generations. My dad grew up on a big dairy farm and after early morning chores that included feeding and milking the cows, the entire family would come inside for a hearty breakfast.

1-1/4 c. sifted enriched flour
1 T. baking powder
1 T. sugar
1/2 t. salt

1 egg, beaten
1 c. milk
2 T. salad oil, melted shortening or bacon fat

Sift flour with baking powder, sugar and salt. Combine egg, milk and shortening, add to dry ingredients. Stir just until flour is moistened, batter will be lumpy. Bake on an ungreased griddle, turning when golden. Makes 6 to 8 cakes.

Kids love pancakes rolled around peanut butter and jelly!

Overnight Apple French Toast

Diane Sullivan
Gowrie, IA

My sister and I live apart from each other, but occasionally we get to sneak in a weekend of fun. We have this dish when we're together. Since it's made the night before, our agreement is that whoever gets up first pops it in the oven and brews the coffee. The wonderful smell of apples baking and coffee brewing is always enough to get anyone up smiling. Serve it with bacon or sausage on the side, or just use fresh orange slices and strawberries.

1 c. brown sugar, packed
1/2 c. butter
2 T. light corn syrup
4 Granny Smith apples, peeled and sliced 1/4-inch thick

3 eggs
1 c. milk
1 t. vanilla
9 slices day-old French bread

In a small saucepan combine brown sugar, butter and corn syrup until thick. Pour into an ungreased 13"x9" pan, arranging apple slices on top of syrup. In a mixing bowl beat eggs, milk and vanilla. Dip French bread in egg mixture and arrange over top of apple slices. Cover and refrigerate overnight. Remove from refrigerator 30 minutes before baking and uncover. Bake at 350 degrees for 35 to 40 minutes, or until the top of the bread is browned.

Sauce:

1 c. applesauce
10-oz. jar apple jelly

1/2 t. cinnamon
1/8 t. cloves

Combine sauce ingredients and cook over medium heat until jelly is melted. Serve French toast with apple slices up and spoon the warm sauce on top. Yum!

Spicy Gingerbread Scones

Jane Kourajian
Lakeville, MN

*Their fragrant aroma warms the cold winter morning air.
Try serving with whipped topping spiced with
cinnamon and nutmeg.*

2 c. flour
3 T. brown sugar
2 t. baking powder
1/2 t. baking soda
1/2 t. salt
1 t. ground ginger
2 t. cinnamon

1/4 t. nutmeg
1/4 c. butter
1 egg yolk, beaten
1/3 c. molasses
1/4 c. milk
1 egg white, beaten
sugar

In a large bowl, stir together first 8 ingredients. Using a pastry blender, cut in butter until mixture resembles coarse crumbs and make a well in the center. In a small bowl, stir together egg yolk, molasses and milk. Add to center of flour mixture and combine with a fork, mixing well. Mixture will be dry in texture. Turn dough onto a lightly floured surface. Quickly knead dough for 10 to 12 strokes or until nearly smooth. Pat into a 7-inch circle and cut into 8 wedges. Arrange wedges one inch apart on an ungreased baking sheet. Brush with egg white and sprinkle with sugar. Bake in a 400 degree oven for 12 to 15 minutes, or until light brown. Best when served warm. You can even save time by mixing the dry ingredients together the night before. Serves 8.

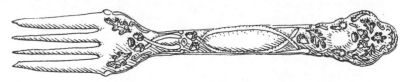

Welcome newcomers to the neighborhood by placing mugs, teabags, coffee, jams, freshly baked bread, muffins or scones in a basket. Tuck in a list of your suggestions for your favorite grocer, doctor, restaurant, repairman and vet.

Rise & Shine

Stuffed French Toast

Kaye Eubanks
West Point, NY

This is the most delicious breakfast I've ever eaten! It's quick, easy, and looks beautiful when topped with fresh seasonal fruit.

8-oz. pkg. whipped cream
   cheese
1 t. vanilla
1/2 c. walnuts, chopped
16 slices white bread

1 c. half-and-half
3 eggs, beaten
1/4 t. nutmeg
1 t. vanilla

Combine cream cheese, vanilla and nuts. Spread on 8 slices of bread and place remaining 8 slices on top to make 8 sandwiches. Cover with wax paper and refrigerate overnight. When ready to prepare, dip sandwiches in half-and-half, eggs, nutmeg and vanilla. Fry on a lightly greased hot griddle.

Sauce:

18-oz. jar apricot jam

1/2 c. orange juice

Heat jam with orange juice, bring to a boil and stir until well mixed. Keep warm and serve with toast.

Your favorite nuts, shelled or unshelled, will keep longer if you store them in the freezer. Nuts that are still in the shell will crack more easily when frozen too.

Gramma's Crumb Cake

Nancy Saimons
Stanwood, WA

A recipe from 1945 that carries on the tradition of warm memories. Our family enjoys this every Christmas morning.

2 c. flour
1 c. sugar
1/2 t. salt
1 t. cinnamon
2 t. baking powder

4 T. shortening
1 egg, lightly beaten
milk
1 t. vanilla
butter

Combine flour, sugar, salt, cinnamon, and baking powder. Cut in shortening, reserve 1/2 cup and set aside. Place beaten egg in a measuring cup and add enough milk to equal one cup. Add vanilla and combine with flour mixture, mixing well. Pour into a greased 8"x8" pan and sprinkle with reserved dry mixture. Dot with butter, sprinkle with sugar and cinnamon. Bake for 25 minutes at 375 degrees. Serves 8.

Too many square meals make too many round people.

- Proverb

Gingerbread Muffins

Anne Daigle
Augusta, ME

Gingerbread muffins are so heart-warming, from the spicy aroma wafting from the oven as they bake to the delicious taste. I remember it because it reminds me of my grandmother's baking and the time I shared with her as a little girl. I make them on special occasions like Christmas, for weekend guests, and as a cure for homesickness. They travel well and have gone to college with my two daughters and been air-mailed to my son stationed in Korea.

2 eggs	2 t. salt
2/3 c. oil	1 t. cinnamon
1 c. molasses	1 t. cloves
1/2 c. sugar	1 t. ginger
3 c. flour	1 c. boiling water
2 t. baking soda	

In a medium bowl beat eggs, oil, molasses and sugar, mixing well. Sift together dry ingredients in a large bowl and add egg mixture. Stir in water, mixing well. Fill greased or paper muffin cups two-thirds full. Sprinkle tops lightly with sugar. Bake in a pre-heated 350 degree oven for 20 to 25 minutes. Makes approximately 2 dozen muffins.

Turn pancakes as soon as they bubble…the pancakes will be tough if you wait for the bubbles to break.

Daddy's Saturday Waffles

Kristi Williams
Gruver, TX

There's nothing like a family breakfast on Saturday morning.

1 c. whole wheat flour
2 t. baking powder
1/2 t. salt
1 t. sugar

1 egg
milk
1/2 c. pecans, chopped

Mix all ingredients together in a bowl. Add enough milk to make a batter of pouring consistency. Cover batter and place in refrigerator overnight. In the morning heat waffle iron, spraying with non-stick cooking spray. Stir batter and pour into waffle iron. Cook until golden. Makes 5 large waffles.

Butter Syrup

Ria Ann Rigby
Malta, ID

This is so scrumptious over a plate of steaming hot pancakes or waffles!

1 can evaporated milk
2 c. sugar

1 T. butter
1 t. vanilla

Combine milk, sugar and butter in a small saucepan, bring to a boil. Add vanilla, stir, serve warm.

Rise & Shine

Old-Fashioned Doughnuts

Cheryl Fancher
Okawville, IL

My aunt used to make these when I was growing up in the 1950's. She would make them on Sunday evenings and invite all my family to her big old farmhouse to share them for supper. The grownups would drink coffee and talk while she made doughnuts, then everyone would dip them in glaze or sugar and eat too many! We children would eat as many raw holes as we later ate cooked. It was always a warm, cozy and loving atmosphere. Today we are calorie and fat conscious and don't make these like in those days, but a batch of these doughnuts and that wonderful smell and taste can transport me back to my childhood.

2 cakes yeast
1 T. sugar
1 c. lukewarm water
1 c. milk
6 T. shortening

1/2 c. sugar
1 t. salt
7 c. sifted flour
3 eggs, beaten

Dissolve yeast and sugar in water. Scald milk, add shortening, sugar and salt. Cool to lukewarm. Add 2 cups of flour to make a batter, add yeast and eggs and beat well. Add remaining flour to make a soft dough. Knead lightly and place in a greased bowl, turning once. Cover and let rise to double in size. Roll out, cut into doughnuts, let rise again. Fry in hot oil until brown. Roll in powdered sugar glaze or sugar.

Doughnuts will be firmer if you allow them to sit for 20 minutes before deep-frying.

Autumn Spice Bread

Lisa Lepak
Suamico, WI

When I was growing up, my mother made this every Thanksgiving and Christmas. The smell of it lingering throughout the house would be a sure sign fall was in the air and would have our family lining up at the oven door! Now my sister and I carry on this scrumptious tradition for our families. Our husbands and kids love this!

3-1/2 c. flour	1/2 t. cloves
2 t. baking soda	1 c. butter
2 t. cinnamon	2 c. sugar
1 t. salt	2 c. canned pumpkin
1 t. nutmeg	4 eggs, lightly whipped
1/2 t. ginger	1-1/2 c. chocolate chips
	1-1/2 c. walnuts, chopped

Grease 2 loaf pans; set aside. Combine flour, soda and spices. Cream butter with sugar and pumpkin, blend in eggs. At low speed add dry ingredients to egg mixture. Mix in chocolate chips and one cup walnuts, stir to blend. Pour into loaf pans and sprinkle with 1/2 cup nuts. Bake at 350 degrees for one to 1-1/2 hours, top with spice glaze. Makes 2 loaves.

Spice Glaze:

1 c. powdered sugar	1/4 t. cinnamon
1/4 t. nutmeg	2 to 3 t. cream or milk
	1/2 c. walnuts, chopped

Combine dry ingredients, blending in cream or milk until mixture becomes the consistency of glaze. Spread on loaves when removed from oven. Sprinkle with remaining nuts. After 5 minutes, remove from pans and cool on a rack.

Sweet Dutch Coffee Cake

Ann Fehr
Trappe, PA

This family recipe is 100 years old.

2 c. flour
2 t. baking powder
1 c. sugar
1/2 c. butter, melted

1 c. milk
2 T. sugar
1 t. cinnamon

Mix flour and baking powder together, set aside. Cream sugar and butter until light and fluffy. Add flour mixture and milk alternately, mixing well after each. Pour into greased 8-inch round pan. Sprinkle with a mixture of sugar and cinnamon. Bake at 350 degrees for 40 minutes.

Preserving Children

Take one large grassy field, 6 children, and 3 dogs. Mix the children with the dogs and empty them into a field, stirring constantly. Sprinkle the entire field with daisies and buttercups, pour a brook gently over pebbles, cover all with a deep blue sky and bake in the sun for several hours. When children are thoroughly browned, they may be removed and set in a bathtub to cool.

-Anonymous

Apple Fritters

Joan Sevcik
Tigard, OR

These were always a special treat growing up. The fall bounty of apples and the smell of cinnamon can't be beat. They're delicious with sausage.

1/2 c. sugar	milk
3 eggs	3 or 4 apples, cored,
dash salt and cinnamon	quartered and thinly
1 c. flour	sliced

Combine sugar, eggs, salt, cinnamon and flour. Add milk until mixture is the consistency of pancake batter. Add apples to batter and stir by hand. Lightly oil a frying pan or griddle. Spoon mixture onto surface to desired size. Fry until golden brown on each side. Sprinkle with cinnamon and sugar and serve warm.

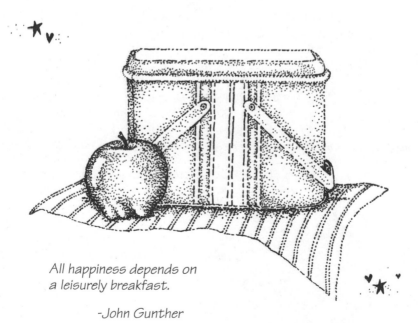

All happiness depends on a leisurely breakfast.

-John Gunther

German Waffles

Blanche Yonk
Petersboro, UT

These German waffles are a keepsake recipe. They remind me of my mom and the smell wafting through her house. I remember my grandmother coming to America from far off Germany and thinking what a long way she had come. I can recall those old waffle irons she brought from far away because Mom had requested she bring them. Now, I am the German waffle maker. They are more than good eating, they are memory makers that not only fill my home with scents of holidays, fond memories of weddings and reunions, but mostly of family.

1 c. plus 2 T. flour	2 eggs, beaten
1 c. milk	1-1/2 t. sugar
1/4 t. salt	powdered sugar
1 t. vanilla or lemon flavoring	

Mix together flour, milk, salt and flavoring, beating until smooth. Add beaten eggs and sugar; stir until creamy. Cover and let stand in refrigerator for one hour, or overnight. When ready to prepare, oil and heat waffle iron. Dip hot iron in batter and fry in hot oil. Shake off excess oil and drain on paper towels. Sprinkle with powdered sugar. Make 40 to 45 waffles.

Every country has their own name for these cookie-like dainties. In Germany they're called German Waffles, in Sweden they are known as Rosettes and in Hawaii they are called Chinese Pretzels. Enjoy!

Raspberry Pull-Aparts

Lori Mulhern
Rosemount, MN

A sweet breakfast treat.

2 loaves frozen sweet roll
    dough or white baking
    dough, partially thawed
3-oz. pkg. raspberry gelatin
1/2 c. white sugar

1/2 c. brown sugar
1 t. cinnamon
1 c. nuts, chopped
1 stick butter or margarine

Thaw dough until just barely soft. Cut each loaf into eight slices, then each slice into four pieces, making 64 pieces in all. Place in a single layer in a well-greased 13"x9" pan. Combine dry gelatin, sugars and cinnamon. Sprinkle over dough, add nuts. Cut butter into slices and distribute evenly over top of dough. Let rise until light, about 30 minutes. Place pan in oven and bake at 350 degrees for 30 to 40 minutes. When done, turn upside down immediately on a serving platter and cool.

To freeze fresh raspberries, coat a cookie sheet with nonstick spray; spread berries on sheet in a single layer and freeze until solid. Remove from tray and place in plastic freezer bags.

Rise & Shine

Blueberry Cream Muffins

Mary M. Warren
Auburn, MI

When our children were small we would always go for adventures in the woods to find wild huckleberries and blueberries. Today we still find places to pick them and they continue to be our family's favorite. They give any meal an old home taste.

2 eggs
1 c. sugar
1/2 c. vegetable oil
1/2 t. vanilla
2 c. flour
1/2 t. salt

1/2 t. baking soda
1 t. baking powder
1 c. sour cream
1 c. blueberries, fresh or
    frozen

Beat eggs, gradually adding sugar. Slowly pour in oil and vanilla. Combine dry ingredients and add sour cream and egg mixture alternately. Fold in blueberries, thoroughly defrost if frozen, and spoon into sprayed muffin cups or paper liners. Sprinkle with topping.

Topping:

2 T. sugar

1 t. cinnamon

Mix topping ingredients together and sprinkle over muffins. Bake at 400 degrees for 20 minutes. Makes 18 to 20 muffins.

Sweet Bread

Karen Moran
Navasota, TX

Sweet Bread reminds me of my childhood watching and helping my mother bake the loaves as Christmas gifts for special friends.

3 pkgs. yeast
2 c. lukewarm water
2 T. sugar
5 lbs. flour
2-1/2 c. sugar
1 T. mace
1 T. salt

1 lb. raisins
13-oz. can evaporated milk
1 c. nuts
3 sticks butter
1/2 c. oil
5 eggs

Dissolve yeast in water, add sugar. Combine with remaining ingredients, mixing well. Place in a large, greased mixing bowl. Turn dough to coat. Set aside and allow to rise for 2 hours, punch down and let rise 2 more hours. Oil and sugar 6 loaf pans, divide bread evenly and place in loaf pans. Let rise 2 hours, then bake at 250 degrees for one hour. Turn off oven, let loaves stand in oven for 15 minutes. Makes 6 loaves.

If the water you add to your yeast is too hot, it will kill the yeast. To test the temperature, pour the water over your forearm. If you cannot feel either hot or cold, the temperature is just right.

Jean's Coffee cake

Deborah Brown
Pasadena, CA

This coffee cake recipe is my favorite because it reminds me of my sister. Every Christmas morning our family would gather at her house for breakfast and to share gifts. Now that she's no longer with us, I continue the tradition of making this coffee cake each Christmas and it always sparks fond memories of her.

1/2 c. butter
1 c. sugar
3 eggs, lightly beaten
1 t. baking powder
1 t. baking soda

2 c. flour
1 c. sour cream
2 c. fresh or frozen
   raspberries

Preheat oven to 350 degrees. Cream butter and sugar, add eggs, baking powder and baking soda. Alternately add flour and sour cream to mixture and fold in raspberries. Pour into a well-buttered bundt pan. Spread with topping.

Topping:

1 c. brown sugar
1/4 c. butter

1/4 c. flour

Combine brown sugar and butter, mixing well. Add flour, mixture will be lumpy. Spread on coffee cake batter, bake for 35 to 45 minutes or until a toothpick comes out clean.

Orange Blossoms

Pat Neaves
Kansas City, MO

A wonderful spicy muffin with marmalade filling!

6 oz. orange juice
  concentrate
3/4 c. sugar
2 T. vegetable oil
1 egg, beaten
2 c. biscuit mix
1/2 c. orange marmalade

1/2 c. pecans, chopped
1-1/2 T. flour
1 t. cinnamon
1/2 t. nutmeg
1 T. butter

Combine orange juice, 1/2 cup sugar, oil and egg in a medium bowl. Add biscuit mix and beat until smooth. Fold in marmalade and nuts. Line muffin tins with paper liners and fill two-thirds full. Combine remaining sugar, flour, cinnamon, nutmeg and butter in a small bowl. Mix with fork until crumbly and sprinkle on top of muffins. Bake at 400 degrees for 20 to 25 minutes. Makes 12 to 15 muffins.

Make raspberry butter quickly by combining one cup butter, 2 cups powdered sugar and 10 ounces frozen raspberries, thawed. Mix until smooth...wonderful!

Rise & Shine

Pumpkin Muffins

Colette A. Chapin
Kansas City, MO

Pumpkin muffins have the most wonderful aroma. They remind me of Thanksgiving, coming home from college and being with my family.

1-1/3 c. sugar
1/2 c. butter
2 eggs
2 c. flour
4 t. baking powder

1 t. cinnamon
1/2 t. salt
1 c. canned pumpkin
4 T. milk

Cream together sugar and butter. Add eggs and beat well. In a separate bowl combine flour, baking powder, cinnamon and salt. In another mixing bowl combine pumpkin and milk. Add flour mixture and pumpkin mixture alternately to creamed mixture, beating well after each addition. Spoon into greased muffin tins and bake at 350 degrees for 18 to 20 minutes. Makes about two dozen muffins.

Old tunes are sweetest and old friends are surest.

- Proverb

Cranberry Nut Bread

Amy Nicol
Marysville, OH

A 4-H fair entry in 1982...I think I prepared it 7 or 8 times for my family in the week prior to the county fair!

2 c. flour	3/4 c. orange juice
1 c. sugar	1 t. orange rind, grated
1-1/2 t. baking powder	1 egg
1 t. salt	1 c. fresh cranberries
1/2 t. baking soda	1 c. nuts
1/4 c. shortening	

Sift dry ingredients and cut in shortening. Combine orange juice, rind and egg. Mix together enough to moisten, carefully add cranberries and nuts. Bake in a lightly greased loaf pan at 350 degrees for one hour.

Quick breads will have a better flavor if you store them overnight before slicing and serving them.

Rise & Shine

Carrot-Raisin Jar Bread

Barbara Hielscher
La Grange, TX

Delicious and great for gift baskets!

2-2/3 c. sugar
2/3 c. shortening
4 eggs
2/3 c. water
2 c. shredded carrots
3-1/2 c. all-purpose flour
1/4 t. cloves

1 t. cinnamon
1 t. baking powder
2 t. baking soda
1 t. salt
2/3 to 1 c. raisins

You'll need 6 wide-mouth pint-size canning jars, metal rings and lids. Don't use any other jars. Sterilize jars, lids and rings according to manufacturer's directions. Grease inside, but not rims of jars. Cream sugar and shortening, beat in eggs and water, add carrots. Sift together flour, cloves, cinnamon, baking powder, baking soda and salt, add to batter. Add raisins and mix. Pour one cup of batter into prepared jars. Do not use more than one cup or batter will overflow and jar will not seal. Place jars evenly spaced on a cookie sheet. Place in a pre-heated 325 degree oven for 45 minutes. Remove jars from oven one at a time keeping remaining jars in oven. Working quickly, wipe rim, place lid and ring on jar and secure. Jars will seal quickly. Repeat with remaining jars. When ready to serve, bread will slide out. A properly sealed quick bread will stay fresh for one year.

Ham, Broccoli & Cheese Quiche
Alicia L. Bates
Kent, OH

For my 20th birthday my Mama, Lorry Bates, gave me an heirloom cookbook. She had various relatives and close friends write out their favorite recipes. I am sure this will be one of my treasured possessions as the years pass. My mom has made this dish for years, it's very good and hearty.

1 c. half-and-half
5 large eggs, beaten
1/2 t. dry mustard
1/4 t. pepper
1 c. cubed ham
1-1/2 c. Cheddar cheese, shredded
1 c. broccoli, blanched and chopped
1 small onion, finely chopped
9-inch pie crust

To make quiche filling, combine half-and-half, eggs, mustard and pepper; set aside. Layer ham, cheese, broccoli and onion into prepared pie crust. Pour egg mixture over ham layers and bake for 45 to 50 minutes in a 350 degree oven. When a knife inserted comes out clean, remove from oven and let cool 5 minutes before slicing.

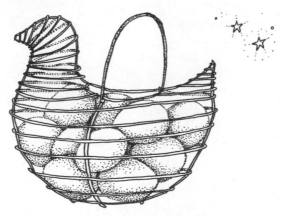

To grate cheese easily, place wrapped cheese in the freezer for 10 to 20 minutes before grating.

Cherry Pecan Bread

Karen Moran
Navasota, TX

My mom always made this for Valentine's Day.

1/2 c. butter
3/4 c. sugar
2 eggs
2 c. flour
1 t. baking soda
1/2 t. salt

1 c. buttermilk
1 c. pecans, chopped
10-oz. jar maraschino
   cherries, chopped and
   drained
1 t. vanilla

Cream butter, sugar and eggs until fluffy. Sift flour, baking soda and salt. Add to creamed mixture alternately with buttermilk. Stir in nuts, cherries, and vanilla. Bake in greased and floured loaf pan for 50 to 60 minutes at 350 degrees. Makes one large loaf or 3 small loaves.

For a change of pace, try serving hot cooked rice with butter, cream and sugar for breakfast. You can even top it with fresh fruit or a dash of cinnamon.

Orange Nut Muffins

Donna Nowicki
Stillwater, MN

These muffins are light, moist and delicious. My kids love them hot out of the oven with a hot cup of fresh apple cider. No butter or spreads are needed. These wonderful muffins are tasty and satisfying anytime.

1 c. butter
1 c. sugar
2 large eggs
1 c. buttermilk

4 T. orange peel, grated
2 c. all-purpose flour
1 t. baking soda
1/4 c. walnuts, chopped

In a large bowl cream butter and sugar beating until fluffy. Blend in eggs. Add buttermilk and orange peel. Beat until well mixed. In a small bowl combine flour and baking soda, stirring to mix. Add to liquid mixture. Blend until just mixed, not over-mixing. Fold in walnuts and spoon mixture into paper-lined muffin tin. Fill two-thirds full and bake for 20 minutes at 350 degrees. While muffins are baking, prepare glaze.

Glaze:

1/2 c. dark brown sugar

1 c. orange juice

Combine ingredients in a small bowl, stirring well. When muffins are removed from oven, spoon glaze directly on hot muffins. Remove muffins to wire rack and cool. Makes 15 muffins.

Rise & Shine

Raisin Muffins

Kathy Williamson
Gooseberry Patch

My daughters, Christie and Amy, love to bake these easy-to-make muffins with me. We enjoy them Sunday morning for breakfast, or even serve them with dinner. The batter will last for 6 weeks in the refrigerator...don't forget to put a date on the container! A wonderful time-saver for any busy family!

1 15-oz. pkg. bran ceral
   with raisins
1 c. margarine, melted
3 c. sugar
4 eggs, beaten

1 qt. buttermilk
5 c. flour
5 t. baking soda
2 t. salt
2 c. boiling water

Mix all ingredients together until well combined. Store in your refrigerator in a covered container for up to 6 weeks. When ready to bake, fill paper muffin cups two-thirds full, bake 15 to 20 minutes at 400.

Kissing don't last, cooking does!

-Proverb

MOM'S
Soup & Sandwich
·SPECIALS·

Our Daily Bread ♡ Some Nice HOT Soup

Shredded Chicken Sandwiches

Doris Stegner
Gooseberry Patch

Whenever there's a social gathering at church these are sure to show up, it seems to be a Midwest tradition! These are wonderful spooned onto soft rolls and served with the classics; potato salad, cole slaw, or baked beans.

1 T. butter
1 onion, diced
1 stalk celery, chopped
1 c. chicken broth
3 boneless, skinless chicken
  breast halves

1 T. cornstarch
1/2 c. milk
salt and pepper to taste

Melt butter in a saucepan and sauté onions, celery and one tablespoon chicken broth. Continue to sauté for 5 minutes, add chicken and remaining broth. Bring to a boil and continue simmering until chicken is tender. Remove chicken from saucepan and allow to cool until it's easily handled. Shred chicken, return to saucepan and bring to a simmer. Combine cornstarch and milk in a small mixing bowl, slowly add to chicken mixture, simmering 5 minutes. Continue to simmer and shred chicken until mixture has thickened but is still moist, approximately 8 minutes. Season with salt and pepper. Makes 5 to 6 sandwiches.

Vegetable Macaroni Soup

Kathy Wienberg
Roselle, IL

This soup is healthy, less than 3 grams of fat, makes my house smell so good and homey while it cooks! Besides all that...it tastes great!

6 c. water, divided
1 c. carrot, sliced
1-1/2 c. onions, chopped
1 T. brown sugar
1/2 t. marjoram
1/2 t. thyme
3 cloves garlic, crushed
28-oz. can chopped tomatoes
1 c. celery, sliced
1 c. dried lentils
1/2 t. basil
3 13-3/4 oz. cans chicken
   broth

1/2 t. oregano
1/2 t. pepper
1 bay leaf
6-oz. can tomato paste
9-oz pkg. frozen green
   beans, thawed
1/4 c. white wine vinegar
1 c. macaroni, uncooked
Romano cheese

Combine all ingredients except 2 cups of water, vinegar and macaroni in a large stock pot and bring to a boil. Cover and reduce heat to simmer for 45 minutes. Add reserved water, vinegar and macaroni and cook for 8 minutes. Remove bay leaf and serve topped with Romano cheese. Makes 17 cups of soup.

If you drop a lettuce leaf into a pot of soup it will absorb the excess grease.

Grandma's Sandwich Buns

Carolyn Glenn
Delaware, OH

These are so wonderfully fresh and worth a little extra effort. If you want to shorten the preparation time, cut the recipe in half and use warm milk.

2 pkgs. dry yeast
1-1/2 c. sugar
2 c. warm water
1 T. salt
1 c. vegetable oil

2 eggs
2 c. milk
11 c. flour
melted butter

Dissolve yeast and 1/2 cup sugar in warm water for 5 minutes. Add salt, remaining sugar and oil to mixture. Beat eggs and milk together then add to yeast mixture. Gradually stir in flour to form a soft dough. Knead dough on a floured surface for 5 to 8 minutes, until smooth and elastic. Place in 2 large greased bowls, cover and allow to rise until double in bulk, 5 to 6 hours. Punch down and let rise until double again, about 2 hours. Using pieces of dough the size of a golf ball, shape into buns, pressing bottom flat onto a greased baking sheet. Let rise an additional 2 hours. Bake at 375 degrees for 15 to 18 minutes. Remove from oven, brush tops with melted butter and cool on a wire rack. Makes 48 buns.

To form hamburger patties in a flash, shape ground beef into a log and freeze it partially. Cut the log into slices, lay on a cookie sheet and freeze until solid. Remove from cookie sheets and place in freezer bags...perfect hamburgers when you're ready for them!

Chicken Stew & Dumplings

Paula Holt
Highland Falls, NY

A favorite because it cooks in one pot, makes the whole house smell delicious and tastes great!

3 onions, quartered
3 stalks celery, cut in 1-inch
    pieces
1 T. butter
1 roasting chicken, rinsed
1 lb. carrots, peeled and cut in
    1-inch pieces

1 bay leaf
salt and pepper
2 T. flour
1/4 c. cold water

In a Dutch oven, brown onions and celery in butter. Brown chicken on all sides, turning breast side down last. Add carrots, bay leaf, salt and pepper to taste. Chicken and vegetables will make their own broth as it cooks. Cover and simmer for 2 hours, stirring occasionally. Cool slightly and remove chicken and bay leaf from pan. Pull meat from bone and return to Dutch oven. Bring stew back to a low boil. Add flour and water mix to thicken gravy. Prepare dumplings.

Dumplings:

2 c. biscuit baking mix   2/3 c. milk

Combine ingredients in a medium bowl. Drop by spoonfuls into bubbling stew. Cook uncovered for 10 minutes, cover and cook for an additional 10 minutes. Remove bay leaf before serving. Serves a family of 5 with leftovers!

God has given us memories, that we might have roses in December.

J.M. Barrie

Reuben Sandwich

*Linda Webb
Gooseberry Patch*

One terrific sandwich! Try it with Russian dressing for a change!

2 slices corned beef
1 slice Swiss cheese
2 slices dark rye or pumper-
    nickel bread

4 T. sauerkraut
1-1/2 T. Thousand Island
    dressing
3 T. butter

Place one slice corned beef and cheese on a slice of bread. Pile on sauerkraut, top with dressing. Put on second slice of corned beef and bread. Melt butter in a skillet over medium heat, and grill sandwich on each side until cheese melts and bread is toasted.

Make wonderful memories; join your neighbors, friends and family in planning a good old-fashioned outdoor potluck. Set up the picnic table, break out the volleyball net, make pitchers of icy lemonade, arrange lots of chairs in the shade and invite everyone to bring their favorite food.

Garden Harvest Chowder

Barbara Elliott
Lititz, PA

Thick, hearty and very warming on a chilly day!

1/4 lb. bacon, finely chopped
1/2 c. celery, chopped
1/2 c. onion, chopped
1/2 c. carrot, peeled and
    thinly sliced
1-1/2 c. water
1/2 c. frozen peas

2 c. potatoes, peeled, cooked
    and mashed
16-oz. can cream-style corn
2 c. milk
1-1/2 c. sharp Cheddar
    cheese, grated
salt and pepper to taste

Fry bacon, celery, onion and carrots in a 6-quart saucepan until bacon is semi-crisp and vegetables are tender. Add water and peas, cook 15 minutes over medium heat until peas are tender. Add remaining ingredients, except cheese. Cook over medium heat, stirring occasionally, until heated through. Add cheese, stirring until melted, but not boiling.

Deviled Ham Spread

Becky Sykes
Gooseberry Patch

A recipe from the 1940's that's perfect anytime. Garnish with lettuce, pickles, olives...whatever you prefer!

2-1/4 oz. deviled ham
1 T. celery, finely chopped
1 hard-cooked egg, chopped
1/4 t. curry powder

1/2 t. olive oil
mayonnaise
salt
paprika

Combine deviled ham, celery and egg. Mix curry powder with olive oil and add to ham mixture. Add enough mayonnaise to make mixture a good spreading consistency. Season with salt and paprika.

Your pastry blender is perfect for slicing hard-boiled eggs or mashing avocados.

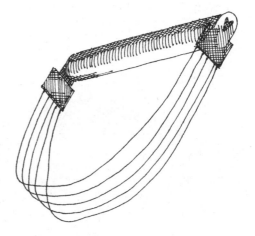

Cream Of Mushroom Soup
Katherine Pope Wyatt
San Francisco, CA

My mother used to make cream of mushroom when I wasn't feeling well. She would say, "Well, it looks like you need some of my cream of mushroom soup and some ginger ale." That was all I needed to get me feeling warm fuzzies inside. It meant love to me to hear her in the kitchen making up a batch of her wonderful soup. It did make me feel a lot better!

3/4 to 1 lb. mushrooms
2 T. olive oil
1/2 medium yellow
   onion, chopped
1 potato, shredded

1 carrot, shredded
1-1/2 qts. chicken broth
1/2 c. barley, rinsed
1 c. half-and-half
2 T. parsley, chopped

Clean and chop mushrooms. Heat one tablespoon of oil in a large skillet. Sauté mushrooms over medium heat until water has evaporated, about 9 minutes; set aside. In a large pot heat remaining oil and sauté onion until transparent. Add potato, carrot and cook over medium heat stirring constantly. Add chicken broth and bring to a low boil. Keep at a steady boil until vegetables are tender. Add mushrooms and barley, simmer for 30 to 40 minutes. Remove about 90% of the vegetable mixture and purée. Stir back into pot; add half-and-half and heat through. Sprinkle with chopped parsley and serve.

Broccoli Cornbread

Jayne Ash
Park Hill, OK

I'm 73, my husband's 75 and we really like this recipe. It's easy and good cold or split and toasted under the broiler with a little slice of cheese. Take it to your next social, you'll get smiles and compliments!

5 eggs, beaten
1 large onion, chopped
10-oz. pkg. frozen broccoli,
    thawed and drained

1-1/2 sticks butter, melted
2 c. cottage cheese
2 7-oz. pkgs. cornbread mix
2 T. sugar

Combine all ingredients and pour into a 12"x9" pan or an 11-inch skillet. Bake for 45 minutes at 350 degrees.

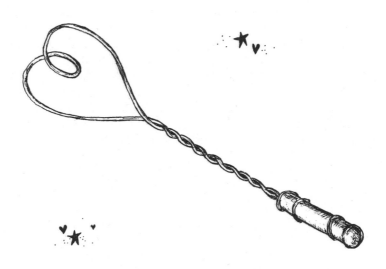

Recycle empty eggshells. Let eggshells dry out, then finely crush in a blender to make bonemeal for plants.

Some nice hot soup

Corn & Shrimp Chowder

Lisa Cook
Amherst, WI

This chowder always brings back memories of family and friends. Our closest friends first served this to my family after a day of skiing. My mother adopted the recipe and has made it the traditional soup to serve when we all gather for a holiday weekend. A steaming hot bowl of this soup and a thick chunk of homemade cornbread is a memorable way to be greeted on a chilly Wisconsin evening!

8 oz. diced salt pork or bacon
   sliced
3 T. green pepper, chopped
1/2 c. celery, chopped
3 T. carrot, diced
2 medium onions, chopped
1 small bay leaf
2 T. flour

4 c. water
3 c. potatoes, diced
17-oz. can creamed corn
1 c. cooked fresh or frozen
   corn
2 c. evaporated milk
1 lb. shrimp, cooked and
   cleaned

In a large soup pot, cook salt pork or bacon until crisp, stirring frequently. Remove meat and pour off all but 3 tablespoons of fat. Add the next five ingredients and sauté 5 minutes. Blend in flour. Add water and potatoes. Cover and simmer 15 minutes. Add remaining ingredients and heat through, remove bay leaf. Sprinkle with salt and pepper. Serve piping hot with a sprinkle of paprika and fresh parsley. Serves 6 to 8.

Club Sandwich

JoAnn

The perfect sandwich! Great when made with freshly baked bread, lots of chicken and thinly sliced tomatoes. Pile it on and make it a lofty sandwich!

2 T. mayonnaise
3 slices fresh bread, toasted
4 thin slices cooked chicken
    breast
salt and pepper to taste

3 thin slices tomato
3 slices bacon, fried crisp
green olives
sweet pickles

Spread mayonnaise on both sides of the toast, cover with chicken, sprinkle with salt and pepper, and cover with slice of toast. Place tomatoes and bacon on top of toast, season again with salt and pepper, cover with last slice of toast. Cut in quarters, diagonally, serve with olives and pickles.

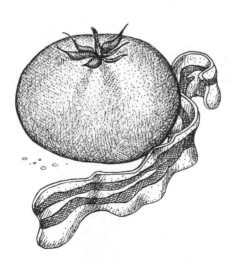

Dip your bacon strips in cold water before frying; this will help keep the ends from curling up.

Velvet Chicken Soup

Kathy Grashoff
Ft. Wayne, IN

This recipe is from a department store tea room in Ft. Wayne. My mom and I would always meet on the top floor and have this for lunch. It's delicious, but sadly, the restaurant is now closed. I'm happy to have this recipe to share.

6 T. butter	3 c. chicken broth
6 T. flour	1 c. chicken, cooked and
1/2 c. milk	chopped
1/2 c. light cream	dash of pepper

In a saucepan melt butter. Blend in flour, stir in milk, cream and chicken broth. Cook over medium heat, stirring occasionally, until mixture thickens and comes to a boil. Reduce heat and stir in chicken and pepper. Return soup to boiling and serve immediately. Makes 5 cups.

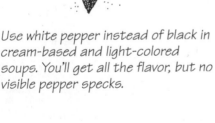

Use white pepper instead of black in cream-based and light-colored soups. You'll get all the flavor, but no visible pepper specks.

Bagels

Kathy Williamson
Gooseberry Patch

Homemade bagels are so soft and chewy. Layer on your favorite spread or sandwich filling, or place a slice of cheese on top and place under the broiler.

2 pkgs. active dry yeast
4-1/4 to 4-1/2 c. sifted flour
1-1/2 c. lukewarm water

3 T. sugar
1 T. salt

In a large mixing bowl, combine yeast and 1-3/4 cup flour; set aside. Combine water, sugar and salt; add to yeast mixture. Beat at low speed, then by hand, stir in enough of the remaining flour to make a moderately stiff dough. Turn on on a lightly floured surface and knead until smooth, 5 to 8 minutes. Cover; let rest 15 minutes. Cut into 12 portions; shape into smooth balls. Flour your index finger and punch a hole in the center of each ball. Pull gently to enlarge the hole, working each bagel into uniform shape. Cover; let rise 20 minutes. In a large kettle, combine one gallon water and salt, bring to a boil. Reduce to simmering and drop bagels in 4 or 5 at time, cooking for 7 minutes, turning once. Drain, place on an ungreased baking sheet and bake at 375 degrees for 30 to 35 minutes. Makes 12 bagels.

GRAPE JELLY

Enjoy the fourth of July outdoors...serve dinner on a lantern-lit porch. Decorate with a basket of mini American flags and Queen Anne's lace, a barrel of red and white geraniums and blue petunias.

Portuguese Stew

Kristine Gilbert
Bath, NY

A sentimental recipe passed down from my Godmother, Paulette, who gave it to my mother, who in turn passed it on to me. What a great, lasting memory and gift!

1 T. olive oil
1 large onion, chopped
1 lb. kielbasa or smoked
   sausage, sliced
1/2 lb. pepperoni, sliced
28-oz. can whole tomatoes

15-oz. can cannellini beans,
   drained
15-oz. can kidney beans,
   drained
15-oz. can chick peas
4 T. vinegar

Heat oil in a large pot; add onion and sauté until tender. Add kielbasa and pepperoni and simmer for 15 minutes. Add tomatoes and bring to a boil. Add cannellini beans, kidney beans and chick peas. Bring to a boil, add vinegar, bring to a boil again. Reduce heat and simmer for 20 to 30 minutes. Easily made in a slow-cooker by combining all ingredients together and simmering on low all day or for 4 hours on high.

Use your kitchen shears to cut canned tomatoes while they're still in the can.

Poor-Boy Sandwich

Vickie

The fillings of this sandwich vary from region to region. In New Orleans the fillings begin with fried potatoes and end with crabmeat, this is the traditional version.

12" loaf French bread
1/2 c. mayonnaise
1 c. shredded lettuce
6 slices roast beef, thinly
    sliced

1/2 c. beef gravy, warm
2 tomatoes, thinly sliced

Split bread lengthwise and warm in the oven. Remove from oven and spread bottom of loaf with mayonnaise, layer with lettuce and beef. Spoon warm gravy over meat and top with tomatoes. Add top half of loaf. Cut into 2 or 3 sections and serve warm. Serves 2 or 3.

To speed tomato ripening, place them in a brown paper bag in a dark closet. The tomatoes will ripen overnight!

Tortilla Soup

Pattye Parker
Edgewood, TX

On cold, cloudy days you will usually find a slow-cooker full of warm tortilla soup in my cozy Texas kitchen. It is one of my favorite recipes because it's easy to prepare and my guests always enjoy it. My two daughters now prepare it for their families.

1 garlic clove
1 medium onion,
4 T. oil
2 cans Mexican-style
    tomatoes, chopped
2 cans stewed tomatoes,
    chopped
4 c. chicken broth

2 c. beef broth
1-1/2 c. chicken, chopped
1 T. cumin
chili powder to taste
10 to 15 corn tortillas, torn
Garnish: cheese, sour cream,
    picante sauce

Sauté garlic and onion in oil. Add tomatoes, broths, chicken, cumin and chili powder, mixing well. Simmer one hour on medium heat, then add torn tortillas. Garnish with cheese, sour cream, or picante sauce.

Enjoy an outing in the crisp air and colorful countryside this autumn. Take along a thermos of hot soup, loaf of crusty bread, and jug of cider.

Yankee Bean Pot Bread

Cyndy Rogers
Upton, MA

Its unusual ingredients make this bread my favorite! It has a wonderful aroma while baking.

6 to 6-1/2 c. all-purpose
   flour
2 pkgs. dry yeast
2 T. brown sugar
1 T. salt
1-1/2 c. water
11-oz. can bean and bacon
   soup, undiluted

2 large shredded wheat
   biscuits
1/4 c. molasses
2 T. butter
2 eggs

In a large mixing bowl, combine 2 cups flour, yeast, brown sugar and salt; mix well. In a saucepan, combine water with soup and crumbled, shredded wheat biscuits, molasses and butter. Heat until warm; butter doesn't need to melt. Add to flour mixture. Add eggs and blend at low speed until moistened; beat 3 minutes at medium speed. By hand, gradually stir in remaining flour to make a firm dough. Knead on floured surface until smooth and elastic, about 5 minutes. Place in greased bowl, turning to grease top. Cover; let rise in a warm place until light and doubled, about one hour. Punch down dough. Divide into two parts. On lightly floured surface, roll or pat each half to a 14"x7" rectangle. Starting with shorter side; roll up tightly, pressing dough into roll with each turn. Pinch edges and ends to seal. Place in greased 9"x5" loaf pans. Cover; let rise in a warm place until light and doubled, about 45 minutes. Bake at 375 degrees for 35 to 40 minutes, or until golden brown and loaves sound hollow when tapped. Remove from pans; brush with butter, if desired. Cool.

Spray your measuring cup with cooking spray before measuring syrup, molasses, or honey. You'll get a more accurate measurement and the cup will wash so much easier!

Baked Potato Soup

Carol Bull
Gooseberry Patch

Served with sourdough bread and herb butter, this is always a favorite in our family!

5 large baking potatoes
1/2 stick butter
1/2 c. flour
7 c. milk
1 bunch green onions, chopped

1/2 lb. bacon, fried crisp and crumbled
1-1/2 c. Cheddar cheese, shredded
1 c. sour cream
salt and pepper to taste

Bake potatoes until tender. Cool, peel and chop into small pieces. Melt butter in a large Dutch oven and stir in flour to make a roux. Slowly whisk in milk, and over medium heat, bring to almost boiling. Add potatoes, green onions and bacon. Stir in cheese and sour cream. Heat through until cheese is melted and soup is warm. Garnish with chopped green onion and crumbled bacon, if desired.

Bring vinegar to a boil in your new saucepan; it will help prevent foods from sticking.

Nissu

Joan P. Morris
Tallahassee, FL

Nothing warms the house or heart like bread. My husband's grandmother was Finnish, and measured the ingredients for her Nissu sweet bread in pinches, handfuls and glubs (the noise a thick liquid makes as it leaves a bottle). This recipe is a combination of watching Grandma Z, a Finnish cookbook's directions and my own adaptations.

2 pkgs. yeast
1/4 c. lukewarm water
1/2 t. salt
1-3/4 c. sugar
1 t. ground cardamom

1 c. milk, scalded
7 to 8 c. flour
5 eggs
1/4 c. butter, melted

Dissolve yeast in water, set aside. Place salt, sugar, cardamom and milk in a large bowl. Add half the flour and beat with an electric mixer or by hand until smooth. Add yeast and beat well. Add eggs, one at a time, beating well after each addition. At this point the dough is heavy and an electric mixer can no longer be used. Add remaining flour and knead well. Divide melted butter into thirds and add one third at a time, kneading well after each addition. Continue to knead until the butter is completely kneaded in and dough doesn't stick to hands. Let rise in a warm place until double in bulk. Roll out as desired and make into loaves, braids, coffee rings, or cinnamon and sugar rolls. Allow to rise again until light. Bake in a 375 degree oven for 20 minutes. Glaze with 1/2 cup powdered sugar and 1/2 cup half-and-half if desired.

Peace and rest at length have come, all the day's long toil is past; and each heart is whispering "Home, Home at last!"

-Thomas Hood

Taco Soup

Shannon Barnhart
Ashley, OH

A great soup for cold days. Serve with warm tortilla chips or some cornbread hot from the oven and you have a meal.

15-1/4 oz. can whole kernel
   Mexican-style corn
15-oz. can black beans,
   rinsed and drained
2 14-1/2 oz. cans chicken
   broth

1-1/2 c. chunky mild salsa
Cheddar cheese, shredded for
   garnish, if desired

Combine corn, beans, broth and salsa in a Dutch oven. Cook over low heat until thoroughly heated. Top with shredded cheese if desired. Makes 7 cups.

If your soup tastes too salty, a raw piece of potato placed in the soup will absorb the excess salt; remove before serving.

BBQ Beef

Helen Murray
Piketon, OH

These sandwiches make a wonderful family meal when served with potato salad or baked beans and potato chips.

3 lbs. beef, cooked and
   shredded
1 medium onion, chopped
1/2 c. green pepper
1/2 c. celery

1/2 c. catsup
1/2 c. barbecue sauce
1 t. mustard
1/4 c. lemon juice
1/2 c. brown sugar

Brown beef, onion, green pepper and celery together for 15 minutes; drain. Add remaining ingredients and simmer for 10 minutes more.

Host a family reunion this year! Plan a full day of activities...horseshoe toss, softball games, three-legged races, and lots of catching up! Dust off the picnic tables, they'll be loaded with simple, down-home favorites, share recipes and memories, take lots of pictures.

Vegetable Soup

Debbie Parker
Gooseberry Patch

My grandma was a wonderful cook. I spent many contented hours in the kitchen watching her make all kinds of yummy things to eat. When I was five, she gave me my first cookbook. It was a paperback cookbook for children that she had purchased at the local five and dime store. I remember the very first recipe we made together...vegetable soup. I still have this cookbook in my cookbook collection. In my opinion this is the best vegetable soup. I hope you enjoy it as much as my family and I do.

8 c. water
2 t. salt
1/4 t. pepper
1 t. sugar
6 carrots, diced
3 stalks celery, diced

4 onions, diced
1/4 cabbage, shredded
1 c. canned tomatoes
4 sprigs parsley
2 beef bouillon cubes

Fill a large pot with water, add salt, pepper, and sugar, bring to a boil. Add vegetables, tomatoes and parsley. Lower temperature to medium and simmer one hour. Add bouillon cubes, remove from heat and stir soup until bouillon is completely dissolved. Serve very hot with crackers.

Freeze summer vegetables to enjoy year 'round. Create a "stew bag" by combining corn, carrots, celery, onion, broccoli, tomatoes and potatoes for hearty winter stews and soups.

Farmhouse Honey-Wheat Bread

Mary Murray
Gooseberry Patch

Nutritious, delicious and freezes well.

1-1/2 c. water
1 c. small curd cottage
   cheese
1/2 c. honey
1/4 c. butter
5-1/2 to 6 c. all-purpose
   flour

1 c. whole wheat flour
2 T. sugar
3 t. salt
2 pkgs. active dry yeast
1 egg

In a saucepan heat water, cottage cheese, honey and butter until very warm, 120 degrees. Combine warm liquid with 2 cups flour and remaining ingredients, beating with an electric mixer for 2 minutes. By hand, add enough flour to make a stiff dough and knead on a well-floured surface until smooth and elastic. Place in an oiled bowl, cover and allow to rise until double in bulk, about one hour. Punch down and shape into 2 loaves, place in 2 oiled 9"x5" loaf pans. Cover and allow to rise for 45 minutes, or until double in size. Bake at 350 degrees for 45 minutes, or until loaves sound hollow when tapped.

A little house, a house of my own, out of the wind's and the rain's way.

-Padraic Colum

Wild Rice Soup

Merrill Sakry
Becker, MN

I make a double batch of this soup every Christmas. Our family…13 children and spouses, 29 grandchildren and one great grandchild, always gather at my in-law's home for Christmas. There's usually none left to bring home!

1/2 c. wild rice
1 lb. bacon
3 T. bacon drippings
3/4 c. celery, chopped
1 c. onion, chopped
1/3 c. green pepper, chopped

2 14-oz. cans chicken broth
4-oz. can mushrooms
2 10-oz. cans cream mushroom soup
1 pt. half-and-half

Wash wild rice thoroughly then boil for 15 minutes. Drain, rinse and set aside. Cut bacon into 2-inch pieces and fry until crisp. Remove from pan and discard all but 3 tablespoons of drippings. Sauté celery, onion and green pepper in bacon drippings until transparent. Transfer to a Dutch oven and add rice, broth, mushrooms, soup and bacon. Cook over low heat for one hour. Before serving pour in half-and-half and heat through.

Oatmeal Bread
JoAnn

A tasty bread and perfect for B-L-T's!

2 c. old-fashioned rolled oats
4 t. salt
1 c. light molasses
1/4 stick butter
4 c. boiling water

1 c. lukewarm water, 110 to 115 degrees
2 pkgs. active dry yeast
10 c. flour

Lightly oil 3 9"x5" loaf pans and set aside. In a large mixing bowl combine oats, salt, molasses and butter; add boiling water. Allow mixture to rest one hour. In another mixing bowl, add one cup warm water and yeast, stirring until dissolved. Add to oat mixture, stirring well. Blend in flour mixing gently. Turn out on a well-floured surface and knead for 10 minutes, or until dough is smooth. Place in a well-oiled mixing bowl, turning dough to cover all sides with oil. Set in a warm, draft-free place and allow to rise until double in bulk. Turn out onto a well-floured surface and divide into 3 sections, shaping each into a loaf. Place in pans and allow to rise again until double in size. Bake at 350 degrees for one hour or until they produce a hollow sound when tapped. Remove from pans and allow to cool.

Make a new neighbor feel welcome by giving a loaf of your homemade bread on a cutting board with a stenciled bread cloth and a set of soup bowls.

Santa Fe Chicken Chili

Elaine Minney
Chillicothe, OH

Our family's favorite because it's so tasty and makes several servings!

2 lbs. chicken breasts, cubed
4 garlic cloves, minced
4 large onions, chopped
4 medium sweet peppers, diced
1/4 c. olive oil
3 T. chili powder
2 t. ground cumin
1/4 t. cayenne pepper

28-oz. can tomatoes, diced
14-1/2 oz. can chicken broth
15-1/2 oz. can kidney beans, rinsed and drained
12-oz. jar salsa
10-oz. pkg. frozen corn
1/2 t. salt
1/2 t. pepper

Sauté chicken, garlic, onions and peppers in olive oil. Add remaining ingredients and simmer one hour. Makes 10 servings.

After a day of fishing, enjoy your favorite supper served by the side of the lake just before sunset.

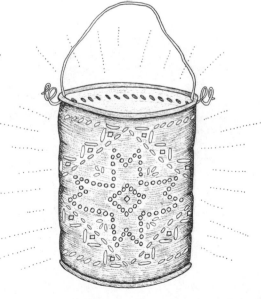

Hero Sandwich

Crystal Parker
Gooseberry Patch

You may call it a hoagie, hero, submarine or grinder, depending on where you live. Add all the ingredients you like, the more the better! For special occasions make it on a 2-foot-long loaf and cut in wedges.

6" French roll
1/4 c. mayonnaise
2-1/2 T. mustard
4 slices cheese: Swiss,
   farmer's, Cheddar,
   provolone

4 slices fully-cooked meat:
   bologna, ham, salami,
   turkey
1 tomato, sliced
1 onion, sliced into rings
pickle slices
shredded lettuce

Split roll lengthwise, top with mayonnaise and mustard. Overlap cheese and meat on roll and add remaining ingredients, replace top of roll. If you want to serve warm, roll sandwich in foil and bake at 350 degrees for 30 minutes.

Mustard

Green onion brushes and curls are a fun addition to your relish plate. To make brushes trim the root end and make 4 or more intersecting slashes at the bulb end; fringe. To make curls, cut green tops lengthwise into several slivers, place in cold water and refrigerate until curled.

Thanksgiving Crab Soup

Monica Vitkay
Bairdford, PA

This soup is a tradition in our family on Thanksgiving day while we're waiting for a late dinner to be prepared. Instead of my family coming in the kitchen in search of snacks, they help themselves to a bowl of nutritious soup. We serve it with corn-bread and it keeps everyone happy until dinner is served! We make the cornbread the evening before Thanksgiving and start the soup early Thanksgiving morning. It's ready for lunch and the tradition begins!

6 c. water
30-oz can beef broth
2-1/2 t. seafood seasoning
1/4 c. onion, chopped
16-oz. can whole tomatoes

20-oz. pkg. mixed vegetables
5 c. potatoes, peeled and sliced
16-oz. can crab meat

Combine water, broth, seasoning and onion in a stockpot and bring to a boil. Add vegetables and simmer 1-1/2 hours. Add crab meat and simmer 1-1/2 hours longer. Serves 6 to 8.

The earliest Thanksgiving feast was recorded at Berkeley Plantation on the James River in December 1619...a year before the Pilgrims landed in Massachusetts.

Cheddar Chicken Salad

Millie Barnhart
Delaware, OH

A favorite from my brother in San Diego, California. He told me to always have the recipe handy because once I served it I'd have many requests for the recipe. It's true! It's always a hit with family, friends and co-workers.

2 c. chicken, cooked and
    chopped
1/2 c. mayonnaise
1/2 c. black olives, chopped
1/2 c. Cheddar cheese,
    shredded

1/4 c. green pepper, chopped
1/4 c. onion, chopped
croissants or pita bread

Combine salad ingredients, mix gently and chill. To serve fill croissants or pita bread.

If you stew a chicken to use later in chicken salads or casseroles, let it cool in its broth before cutting it into chunks…it will have twice the flavor.

Mom's Chicken Soup

Barbara Bargdill
Gooseberry Patch

My mother sent me this recipe when I was first married. Then, when I made it, I felt very close to home, as I knew it's Mom's very own recipe. I loved looking at her beautiful handwriting on a page torn from her notebook. Now, years later, I still love to make this soup. It's so soothing when someone isn't feeling well, a wonderful remedy for colds and flu! Over the years this recipe has been shortened, condensed, or otherwise altered depending on how many children I had running about, or how much time I had. Sometimes though, I just like to prepare it Mom's way. I love to get out and follow the worn original recipe, even though I know it by heart.

1 whole chicken
1 large onion, peeled and
    quartered
4 or 5 carrots, peeled and
    quartered
5 chicken bouillon cubes

1 c. Acine de Pepe pasta, or
    other small pasta
1 egg
1 T. Romano cheese, grated
salt and pepper to taste

Rinse chicken and remove skin, neck and giblets. Place chicken and neck in a large pot and cover with water. Bring to a boil and discard that water. Fill again with cold water and return to a low boil. Add onion and carrot pieces. Cover and boil about one hour. Add bouillon cubes and continue to simmer another half-hour. Skim fat from broth. When meat is tender and falls easily from bone, remove pot from heat. Transfer the chicken to a large bowl and cool slightly. Discard the neck. Remove the onion and carrot pieces from broth and place them in a blender. Add enough broth just to cover. Place lid on blender and pulse for a few seconds. Return vegetable mixture to broth and bring to a simmer and add pasta. Remove chicken from bones, dice and return to broth and continue to simmer. Beat egg in a small bowl and add salt and pepper. Spoon in a small amount of hot broth to egg mixture, add cheese. Slowly pour the egg mixture into simmering soup, beating constantly with a whisk. Salt and pepper to taste, cover pot with a lid and let soup sit 15 minutes before serving.

Country Potato Bread

Vickie

So soft with a wonderful aroma. Great for sandwiches!

1/2 lb. potatoes, peeled and
   sliced
1 pkg. active dry yeast
1/3 stick butter, melted

2 t. salt
1 T. sugar
7 to 9 c. all-purpose flour

Place potatoes in a pan, cover with water and boil until tender. Drain, reserving water and mash. Allow potato water to cool until warm. In a large mixing bowl stir 3 cups of warm potato water and yeast, allow to stand 2 minutes. Add potatoes, butter, salt and sugar, mixing well. Combine potato mixture with 7 cups of flour, enough to produce a workable dough. Blend thoroughly. Knead for 3 minutes on a floured surface, allow to rest 10 minutes, knead again until smooth. Add flour as necessary to keep bread from sticking to surface, form a ball. Lightly oil a large mixing bowl and place dough inside. Rotate ball once to cover completely with oil. Cover bowl with a cloth and allow dough to rise until double in size, about one hour. Punch dough down and knead 2 minutes, divide into 2 balls.

Shape dough into loaves and place in 2 lightly oiled loaf pans. Cover pans and allow loaves to rise until double in size, approximately 45 minutes. Bake in a 350 degree oven for 40 to 45 minutes. Remove from pans and allow to cool before slicing.

Pea Soup

Roxane Gilbert
Berrien Springs, MD

A nice change! Great for a cool autumn day.

1 c. dried whole peas
1 c. dried split peas
4 qt. water
2-1/2 c. onion, chopped
1 c. celery, chopped
2 carrots, cubed

1/2 c. fresh parsley
3 potatoes, cubed
1 t. thyme, dried
1/2 t. chili powder
1 lb. Polish sausage, cooked
   and sliced

Rinse and drain peas well. Put in a stockpot with water, add onion, celery, carrots and parsley. Bring to a boil and simmer uncovered 4 hours, stirring frequently. Add potatoes, thyme and chili powder. Simmer uncovered one hour, add sausage, salt and pepper to taste. Serve when sausage is completely heated. Makes 10 servings.

Place your onions in the freezer for 5 minutes before slicing them;
no more tears!

Onion Bread

Doris Stegner
Gooseberry Patch

This recipe is easily doubled and keeps fresh for a long time.
The onion flavor is light and is wonderful with soups and stews.

1 pkg. active dry yeast
1-1/4 c. warm water
1 c. milk, scalded
2 T. butter
2 T. sugar

1 T. salt
1/2 c. chives
1/4 c. poppy seeds
6 c. flour

In a large mixing bowl, dissolve yeast in 1/4 cup of warm water and allow to stand 10 minutes. In a small bowl, combine milk, remaining water, butter, sugar and salt, mixing well and adding to yeast mixture. Add chives, poppy seeds and one cup flour. Add 1-1/2 cups of flour at a time until dough is stiff and begins to pull away from the sides, approximately 2-1/2 cups total. Turn dough onto a floured board and knead 2 more cups of flour in. Shape dough into a ball, place in an oiled mixing bowl, rotating once to cover ball with oil. Allow to rise until doubled, punch down and form two loaves. Place loaves in oiled 9"x5" pans and bake at 425 degrees for 15 minutes. Reduce heat to 350 degrees and bake for an additional 25 to 30 minutes.

Miniature market baskets are perfect for delivering your homemade bread to a special friend. Stencil a pattern on the handle, line the basket with some homespun and tuck in your loaf of bread.

Autumn Soup

Joanne Marchetti Quinn
San Francisco, CA

This soup evokes memories of my favorite season of the year. It is quick and easy to prepare and looks especially festive in a hollowed-out pumpkin.

1 c. onion, chopped
3 T. butter
16-oz. can pumpkin
10-1/2 oz. can condensed
   chicken broth
2 c. water

1/2 c. instant mashed potato
   flakes
2 t. dried parsley
1/2 to 1 t. dried dill
1/4 t. pepper

In a large saucepan, sauté onions in butter until tender. Add pumpkin, broth and water; mix well and bring to a boil. Reduce heat and simmer for 10 minutes, stirring occasionally. Stir in potato flakes, parsley, dill and pepper. Simmer 5 minutes, stirring frequently.

Topping:

1/4 c. low-fat plain yogurt   dash nutmeg

In a small bowl combine yogurt and nutmeg, mixing well. Ladle soup into serving bowls; spoon scant tablespoon of topping onto each serving.

Grilled Chicken Salad

Linda Lee
Lilburn, GA

A special "ladies" lunch! Prepare this for your best friend on a warm spring or summer day.

2 chicken breasts, boneless
8-oz. bottle Italian salad
   dressing
basil, salt & pepper to taste
mixed green salad leaves

Feta cheese
6 cherry tomatoes
poppy seed dressing

Marinate chicken breast for 15 minutes in Italian dressing. Sprinkle basil and pepper on both sides. Grill or broil chicken breast about 6 minutes per side until thoroughly cooked. Refrigerate chicken until cold then slice into strips. Arrange lettuce leaves on serving plates and place chicken slices on top. Garnish with crumbled cheese and cherry tomatoes. Sprinkle again with basil, salt and pepper. Before serving drizzle with poppy seed dressing. Great when served with tall glasses of iced tea, croissant rolls and tea cookies for dessert. Serves 2.

During the summer, gather and dry armfuls of flowers. The following fall and winter you can enjoy wonderful dried bouquets.

Milk & Cookies, Snacks & more

A little something to tide you over

Old-Fashioned Cocoa

Shannon Barnhart
Ashley, OH

You'll never go back to instant cocoa again!

1/2 c. unsweetened Dutch-
   processed cocoa
1/4 c. powdered sugar
1/2 c. half-and-half

4 c. milk
1 t. vanilla
garnish: grated chocolate and
   whipped cream

In a small saucepan, combine cocoa and sugar, whisk in half-and-half until mixture is smooth. Over low heat, whisk in milk and vanilla, bring to a simmer. Pour into hot mugs and top with whipped cream and grated chocolate if desired. To add variety, add cinnamon and nutmeg before adding milk, or use peppermint extract in place of the vanilla. Makes 4 servings.

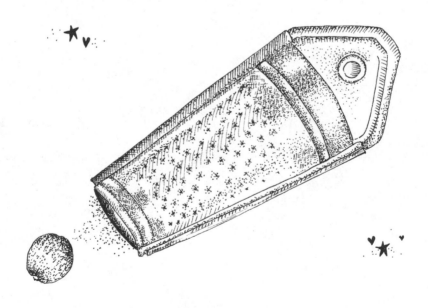

Top your hot cocoa, ice cream soda, or milk shake with a spoonful of sweetened whipped cream. Sprinkle lightly with ground cinnamon, nutmeg, or chocolate shavings.

Moon Cookies

Mary Beth Smith
St. Charles, MO

This was my grandmother's favorite Christmas cookie recipe. It was passed down to her from her mother and grandmother. My grandmother passed away in 1976 and not a day goes by that I don't think of her. Baking her Moon Cookies always makes me feel close to her. Making these every Christmas is a tradition my four daughters and I look forward to. It gives me an opportunity to tell them about how wonderful their great-grandmother was.

1/2 lb. almonds, ground	9 T. sugar
1 lb. butter, room temperature	4 c. flour
	1-1/2 c. powdered sugar

Pre-heat oven to 350 degrees. Place ground almonds on a cookie sheet and bake until golden brown, approximately 5 to 7 minutes. Remove from oven and set aside. Combine butter, sugar and flour. Add cooled, toasted almonds to dough. Mix well with hands and knead dough. Form a ball and place on wax paper, wrap well and refrigerate for one hour. When ready to bake, use 1-1/2 tablespoons of dough rolled into a ball then shaped into a crescent. Place on an ungreased baking sheet and bake at 350 degrees for 9 to 12 minutes, until very lightly golden brown. Remove from baking sheet and let cool. When completely cool, roll each cookie in powdered sugar coating well. Makes 3 to 4 dozen cookies.

When storing cookies, separate the layers between sheets of wax paper to keep crisp cookies crisp and soft cookies chewy.

Mamoul

Antoinette Abdo-Whelpton
Scottsville, NY

This is the first cookie I remember my grandmother making for special occasions. Every Christmas I prepare a special tin for my dad with these cookies. He always says, "They taste just like Mama's."

2 c. butter
2-1/2 c. sugar
6 c. flour
1 c. milk, lukewarm

3 c. ground walnuts
1 t. orange blossom or rose
   blossom water
powdered sugar

Mix butter, 1-1/2 cups sugar and flour, using your hands if necessary. Add milk and mix with a wooden spoon. Roll this mixture on a well-floured pastry cloth and cut into round shapes. In a mixing bowl combine walnuts, remaining sugar and water; set aside. Place spoonfuls of filling in the center of each pastry circle; fold in half and pinch edges. Place on a lightly greased cookie sheet and bake at 350 degrees for 15 to 25 minutes. Cool on a rack, sprinkle with powdered sugar. Makes 6 to 7 dozen cookies, depending on the size.

If your unbaked cookie dough dries too quickly, restore the moisture by placing the dough on a wire rack suspended over a pan of water. Allow the dough to sit for 2 minutes.

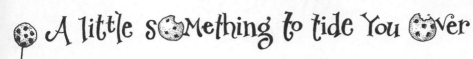

Grandma Martha's Cookies

Martha L. Quintenz
Decatur, IL

I remember I started making these cookies about 20 years ago. My daughters were 5 and 2 and we made them together. When they started school and I was room mother, I always made these cut-outs for all the holidays. One spring our ladies group from church had a salad luncheon and I used this recipe to make 12 dozen flower-shaped cookies...there wasn't one to bring home! They're my favorite because they're enjoyed by everyone who eats them.

1-1/2 c. sugar
1 c. butter, room temperature
2 eggs
1-1/2 t. clear vanilla

3 c. all-purpose flour
1/4 t. baking powder
1/4 t. baking soda

In a large bowl, mix sugar, butter, eggs and vanilla until creamy. Add flour, baking powder and baking soda. Chill dough for 30 minutes. Roll dough on a floured surface to 1/4-inch thickness. Cut with your favorite cookie cutters, dipped in flour. Place on an ungreased cookie sheet at 350 degrees for 10 to 14 minutes. Cool and spread with your favorite icing, or leave plain.

Homemade cookies will stay fresh for up to 2 months in your freezer stored in freezer bags and tucked in airtight containers. When ready to serve, just thaw for 30 minutes.

Russian Tea

Suzanne Wyatt
Snellville, GA

Russian Tea is my favorite recipe because it brings back such wonderful Christmastime memories of cold winter evenings at my grandparents' home in Canton, NC. Lots of family would gather at my grandparents' home to sit in their kitchen and sip warm Russian Tea and munch on homemade Christmas cookies. We shared stories, young and old alike. Nannie always made Russian Tea only during the holiday season and she always had lots for us kids to drink. I am carrying on the tradition during the holidays. Christmas always brings my wonderful memories of Nannie back to mind for she has left us for a better place. I toast you Nannie for your Russian Tea tradition.

16 c. water
2 c. sugar
1 t. whole cloves
3 teabags

1 lg. can pineapple juice
1 frozen can orange juice
   concentrate
juice of 3 lemons

Boil 8 cups of water, sugar and cloves for 5 minutes. Boil remaining 8 cups of water with teabags. Remove cloves and teabags and combine liquids. Add juices and refrigerate.

Instant Russian Tea

1/2 c. instant tea with lemon
2 c. instant orange drink mix

1-1/2 c. sugar
1 t. cinnamon

Sift all ingredients together thoroughly and store in airtight containers. Wonderful for gift giving!

Tint your ice cubes to make your cold drink even better! Mix 2 tablespoons of maraschino cherry juice or a few drops of food coloring with the water in the ice cube tray; freeze.

White Sugar Cookies

Martha E. Taylor
Schoolcraft, MI

*My great-grandmother's recipe and a delicious Christmas
tradition in our family for years.*

2/3 c. shortening
1 c. sugar
2 eggs
1/2 t. vanilla
2 t. baking powder

1/3 c. milk
3 c. flour
1/2 t. salt
sugar and cinnamon, if
    desired

Cream shortening and sugar together, add remaining ingredients
and chill. Roll out on a lightly-floured board, and cut into
desired shapes. Sprinkle with sugar and cinnamon before
baking, or leave plain to frost. Bake at 375 degrees for 6
minutes, makes 2 dozen cookies.

*Cookies can be rolled to 1/4" thickness and baked for less than the
specified time. This will give you a chewier cookie.*

Dad's Sweet Buttermilk Cookies
Janet C. Myers
Reading, PA

The only cookie I was allowed to eat for breakfast! These cookies are so wonderful...so soft and sweet. As a child my mother always took them on our vacation to the beach and I continue this tradition with my family. To this day my 82 year-old mother usually has a batch of Dad's favorite cookies in the freezer, nothing pleases him more.

2 c. sugar	1 t. baking powder
1 c. solid shortening	dash of salt
3 eggs	1 c. buttermilk
4 c. sifted flour	2 t. vanilla
1 t. baking soda	sugar for sprinkling

Cream sugar and shortening; add eggs. Sift dry ingredients and add alternately with buttermilk. Add vanilla. Drop by tablespoonfuls onto a greased cookie sheet and sprinkle with sugar. Bake at 375 degrees for 8 to 10 minutes.

Allow cookie sheets to cool completely before using them for the next batch.

Frosted Maple Cookies

Jana Warnell
Kalispell, MT

During the last half of August when the weather is unbearably hot, I always look forward to the fall and cooler weather. Like so many people I love autumn, so when I start to yearn for that season, I bake a batch of these cookies. They taste of fall and are especially good with a glass of milk or apple cider. They always cure my longing for autumn.

1 c. brown sugar
1 t. maple extract
1/2 t. vanilla
1 egg

3/4 c. butter
1-1/2 c. flour
1 t. baking soda

Combine brown sugar, maple extract, vanilla, egg and butter together. Add flour and baking soda, dough will be very sticky. Drop by teaspoonfuls onto greased cookie sheet. Bake for 10 to 12 minutes at 350 degrees. Let rest one minute before removing from cookie sheet. Frost when cool.

Frosting:

2 c. powdered sugar
2 T. milk

2 T. butter
1 t. maple extract

Combine frosting ingredients and spread over cooled cookies.

Always sift your dry ingredients together; baking soda has a tendency to lump when unsifted.

Cinnamon Spice Cider

*Stephanie McAtee
Kansas City, MO*

This recipe brings back special memories of my mom. I remember it because when I would go home on a crisp autumn night or a cold winter evening, my mom always had a pot of cinnamon spice cider on the stove ready for company and conversation. The aroma always takes me back home.

2 qts. apple cider
1-1/2 qts. cranberry juice
1/4 c. brown sugar

1 orange, sliced
5 cinnamon sticks
1 teaball full of whole cloves

Combine all ingredients in a large stockpot; simmer. Serve warm with a cinnamon stick and an orange slice.

It is extraordinary how music sends one back into memories of the past - and it is the same with smells.

-George Sand

Chewy Granola Bars

Laura Flournoy
Columbus, NC

These are great for lunch snacks or for dessert served warm with ice cream. I sometimes substitute 1/2 cup of cocoa for half of the flour for an extra chocolate delight! My husband says he knows I love him when I send these in his lunch.

1/2 c. margarine, softened
1 c. brown sugar
1/4 c. sugar
2 T. honey
1/2 t. vanilla
1 egg
1 c. flour
1 T. cinnamon

1/2 t. baking powder
1/4 t. salt
1 c. quick oats
1-1/4 c. puffed rice cereal
1 c. nuts
1 c. raisins
1 c. chocolate chips

Cream margarine, sugars, honey, vanilla and egg, mixing well. Combine all dry ingredients and add to creamed mixture. Press into a greased 13"x9"x2" baking pan and bake at 350 degrees for 22 to 28 minutes. Let cool, cut into bars. You can substitute peanut butter chips or butterscotch chips for the chocolate if you like.

Plump up your raisins by covering them with very warm water and allowing them to sit for 15 minutes. Drain, then let the raisins stand for 4 hours before using.

Ethel's Lemon Sugar Cookies

Yvonne Boozel
McVeytown, PA

When I was a child, my grandmother Ethel would make these delicious cookies with my sister and me. We always seemed to make them around Christmas time when the snow was falling. We would mix the dough and put it in the refrigerator to chill, then we would get all bundled up and go out in the snow. We would sled while she watched, then we would get her on the sled and push her around the yard. After all the fun we would go back in the house to warm up. Grandma would take the dough out of the refrigerator and roll out the dough and let my sister and me cut out the cookies. What fond memories I have of my grandmother that I hold so dear to my heart.

3/4 c. shortening
1 c. sugar
2 eggs
1/2 t. lemon flavoring

2-1/2 c. flour
1 t. baking powder
1 t. salt

Mix shortening, sugar, eggs and flavoring thoroughly. Stir flour, baking powder and salt together, blend and chill at least one hour. Heat oven to 400 degrees, roll dough 1/8-inch thick on a floured board and cut with cookie cutters. Place on an ungreased baking sheet and bake 6 to 8 minutes, or until cookies are a delicate golden color.

Sour Cream Cookies

*Carol Hill
Cloquet, MN*

*My mother, who's 93 now, always made these for our family
and then for her grandchildren.*

2 c. sugar
1 c. butter
1 c. sour cream
3 eggs

1 t. salt
1/8 t. nutmeg
1 t. baking soda
6 c. flour

Cream sugar and butter together, add remaining ingredients, blending well. Roll dough out on a floured surface and cut with your favorite cookie cutters. Bake at 350 for 8 minutes, or until lightly golden. When cool, frost with your favorite icing.

If your cookie dough is well-chilled it will roll easily on a floured surface without using plastic wrap or a pastry cloth.

Ginger Beer

Lynette McCartney
Queensland, Australia

When we were kids, Mum would make crates of ginger beer and serve it icy cold on the long hot summer days we have here in Queensland. After playing cricket or swimming, it would be the best thing we looked forward to the most! Now I make it for my children and they love it just as much.

1 t. compressed yeast	1 t. ground ginger
1 t. sugar	1 c. warm water

Put yeast in a 1/2-litre jar, add sugar, ginger, water and mix well. Cover with muslin or cheesecloth and leave for eight days. Add an extra teaspoon of ginger and sugar each day. The contents are now called a "plant".

To make ginger beer:

7 liters water (28 c.)	1/2 c. lemon juice, strained
2 lbs. sugar	

Combine sugar and five cups of water in a large saucepan. Heat until boiling and sugar is dissolved. Remove from heat and add remaining water and lemon juice, stir. Strain "plant" through strainer lined with two thicknesses of muslin. Add liquid to contents of saucepan, stirring well. Pour through a funnel into 8 clean bottles, stirring mixture, as sediment settles quickly, then seal. I use recycled plastic soft drink bottles with screw tops. Ginger beer is ready when bubbles rise to the surface, in about five days. You can release the pressure if it becomes too much by loosening the screw tops.

To make additional plants, divide the remaining sediment in the muslin in half. Put into two jars. To each jar add one cup warm water and one teaspoon each of sugar and ginger. Proceed as before to make two plants. Give one to a friend with the recipe attached!

Clothespin Cookies

Christi Miller
New Paris, PA

This recipe comes from a dear friend who came to America from Italy when she was only 16. She worked hard through the Depression and raised a beautiful family. She was quite the business woman and founded a restaurant that people traveled to from far away to dine in. Everyone adored her. Twenty years later, I often think of all she taught me, not only in the kitchen, but how to be strong and loving as well. Nana lived to be 96 years old, and her three granddaughters and I still remain close. There isn't a time when we meet that we don't recall one of Nana's stories, or laugh at the good times. She never knew when she came to America, that she would touch so many lives, and hearts.

3-1/2 c. flour
2 T. sugar
1 lb. solid shortening

2 egg yolks
1-1/2 c. water

Sift together flour and sugar, cut in shortening. Add egg yolks and water, mixing well. Roll dough out to 1/4-inch, and spread both sides with shortening. Fold up dough and refrigerate for one hour. Unfold dough and spread with shortening again. Return to refrigerator and chill one hour. Repeat again. Roll out dough and cut into strips. Wrap on foil-covered round clothespins and bake at 425 degrees until light brown. Remove cookie from clothespin while still hot, let cool. Pipe filling inside.

Filling:

1 c. milk
4 T. flour
1 c. shortening

2 c. powdered sugar
12 T. marshmallow cream
1 T. vanilla

Combine milk and flour over medium heat until thick. Add remaining ingredients and beat until fluffy. Using a pastry bag fitted with a star tip, fill cookie. Dip ends in sprinkles.

Grandpa's Oatmeal Cookies

Pearl Stahl
Worthington, IN

As children we always loved going to our grandparent's home. It was a special bonus knowing Mom-Mom always had home-made cookies in her cookie jar which was a big white cow sitting on her haunches with a removeable head. That cookie jar now sits in a place of honor on my kitchen counter. The cookies we loved best were the oatmeal and they were the size of a saucer! When I asked for the recipe, Mom-Mom shared the secret that this cookie recipe had been perfected by my Grandpa John. He worked with this recipe until he had an oatmeal cookie that he truly liked. Today these remain my husband's and two daughter's favorite cookie.

1 c. boiling water
1 lb. raisins
1 t. baking soda
1 c. brown sugar
1 c. shortening
2 eggs
2 c. flour

1 T. baking powder
pinch salt
2 t. cinnamon
4 c. quick oats
1 c. coconut
1 t. vanilla

Pour water over raisins, add baking soda, cover and let stand. Cream brown sugar and shortening, add eggs and mix well. Sift flour, baking powder, salt and cinnamon. Add oats, coconut, vanilla and raisin mixture, blend thoroughly. Drop by tablespoonfuls onto a greased cookie sheet and bake at 350 degrees for 12 to 15 minutes. Makes 1-1/2 to 2 dozen cookies.

If you give your cookies as gifts, unique containers can be found at antique shops or garage sales. Look for decorative tins, jars, boxes or dishes to make your home-baked goodies extra special.

Raspberry Cheesecake Bars

Pat Habiger
Spearville, KS

This recipe is a keeper! The layers of cheesecake and raspberry filling combine with the almond crust for a wonderful taste surprise!

1-1/4 c. flour
1/2 c. brown sugar
1/2 c. almonds, finely
  chopped
1/2 c. shortening
2 8-oz. pkgs. cream cheese,
  softened

2/3 c. sugar
2 eggs
1/2 t. almond extract
1 c. seedless raspberry
  preserves or jam
1/2 c. coconut
1/2 c. almonds, sliced

In a mixing bowl, combine flour, brown sugar and almonds. Cut in shortening until mixture resembles fine crumbs. Set aside 1/2 cup of crumb mixture for topping. To make crust, press remaining crumb mixture into bottom of 13"x9"x2" baking pan. Bake in a 350 degree oven for 12 to 15 minutes or until edges are golden. In another mixing bowl, beat cream cheese, sugar, eggs and almond extract until smooth. Spread over hot crust and return to oven for 15 minutes. Spread preserves over cheese mixture, set aside. In a small bowl combine reserved crumb mixture; coconut and sliced almonds; sprinkle over preserves. Return to oven and bake 15 minutes longer. Cool in pan on a wire rack, chill for 3 hours before cutting into bars, store in refrigerator. Makes 32 bars.

To soften brown sugar that's hard, add a few drops of water in the box and microwave for 15 seconds, watching carefully or the sugar will melt.

Banana Smoothie

Kathy Williamson
Gooseberry Patch

Great served as an after-school snack or on hot summer days.

4 ripe bananas
3 c. milk
1/2 c. whipping cream

2 t. vanilla
vanilla ice cream

Whip bananas, milk, cream and vanilla together in a blender until smooth. Serve in tall glasses with a scoop of vanilla ice cream and a banana slice on the edge of each glass as a garnish. Makes 4 servings.

Cool off your favorite summer beverage with frosty glasses. Pour 1/4 cup fruit juice into a shallow bowl, place 1/4 cup of sugar on a section of wax paper. Holding each glass at the bottom, dip rim of glass into juice then into sugar. Set glasses upright in the refrigerator or freezer to chill for 1/2 hour.

Ultimate Chocolate Brownies

Aileen Leaton
Bethlehem, PA

A brownie-lovers delight! You can't eat just one,
they are heavenly.

3/4 c. cocoa
1/2 t. baking soda
2/3 c. butter, melted
1/2 c. boiling water
2 c. sugar
2 eggs

1-1/3 c. flour
1 t. vanilla
1/4 t. salt
1/2 c. pecans, chopped
2 c. semi-sweet chocolate
    chunks

In a large bowl, combine cocoa and baking soda; blend in 1/3 cup of melted butter. Add boiling water and stir until well blended. Mix in sugar, eggs and remaining butter; stir, blend in flour, vanilla and salt. Stir in pecans and chocolate chunks. Pour into a greased 13"x9" pan and bake at 350 degrees for 35 to 40 minutes. Makes 3 dozen brownies.

A fun way to give brownies is to cut them with metal cookie cutters
after they've cooled. Use special cutters for the holidays such as
bunnies, hearts, pumpkins, or bells.

Orange Cookies

Jo Ann Drawdy
Ocoee, FL

I remember my grandmother making these cookies when I was a little girl. I couldn't wait to sneak a taste of the batter and lick the beaters from the frosting. I really don't know if my grandmother put this recipe together for herself or if it was passed on to her; however after I married and started my own recipe collection this was one recipe that immediately came to mind that I wanted to have. These cookies are my favorite because they're a hit anytime of the year. While I most enjoy making them during the holidays, I have also made them to serve at showers and to enjoy in the summertime with home-made ice cream.

4-1/2 c. all-purpose flour	3 eggs
1 t. baking soda	juice and rind of 2 oranges
1 c. shortening	(to equal 1 cup)
2 c. sugar	1 c. buttermilk

Combine flour and baking soda and set aside. Mix together shortening, sugar and eggs and mix well. Stir in orange rind and juice. Add flour mixture and buttermilk, beginning and ending with dry ingredients. Drop by teaspoonfuls onto lightly greased cookie sheet. Bake at 375 degrees for 10 to12 minutes. Cool on wire rack and frost with orange frosting.

Orange Frosting:

1 stick butter   1 box powdered sugar
juice and rind of 1 orange

Cream frosting ingredients together until smooth. If mixture is too stiff add a little more orange juice. Frost cookies after they're completely cooled.

Rachel's Apricot Mumbles

Mary E. Dungan
Gardenville, PA

The week between Christmas and New Years we have family and in-laws, sometimes numbering 40, for dinners and break-fasts. I have many favorite recipes, but this one is so tasty and easy to prepare during the busy holiday season.

3/4 c. butter, softened	1/2 t. baking soda
1 c. brown sugar	1-1/2 c. oats
1-1/2 c. flour	12-oz. jar apricot preserves
1/2 t. salt	

Combine butter and sugar, add flour, salt and baking soda, mix well. Add oats, blending thoroughly. Press half of the dough into a greased 8-inch square pan, spread preserves on top and crumble remaining dough and sprinkle over preserves. Bake at 350 degrees for 25 minutes. Cool and cut into squares.

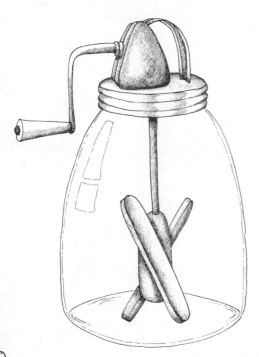

Another easy trick to make hard brown sugar soft again is to place a slice of soft bread in the package; it only takes a couple hours!

Frosty Orange Creamsicle

Molly Bordonaro
Worthington, OH

So cool and refreshing!

6-oz. frozen orange juice
    concentrate
1 c. water
1/4 c. sugar

1/2 t. vanilla
1 c. milk
1 c. ice cubes

Combine all ingredients in a blender until smooth. Serve immediately or freeze until ready to serve. Makes 6 servings.

Serve cold fruit drinks with a fruit kabob in each glass by simply spearing two or more pieces of fruit on a wooden pick. Maraschino cherries, pinapple chunks, apple slices, orange wedges, or fresh strawberries work well.

Vis' Peanut Butter Bars

Terri Vanden Bosch
Rock Vally, IA

These bars bring back so many memories. My Dad was a farmer and farmed with his dad. Every Saturday at 3:30 it was coffee time at Grandma's house and the men would discuss the crops and animals. We'd be treated to these delicious bars and fresh, cold milk straight from the bulk tank, which stores milk after it comes from the cow and before the truck comes to get it. Even cousins that lived in town would come home on Saturday for coffee. It was always a lot fun for the kids, and Grandma would always worry that she would run out of peanut butter bars. These bars were also a great bargaining tool in grade school. We had no hot lunches and had to take dinner pails, so whenever Mom put these in my pail I could always check with the other kids to see if they had anything I wanted. Everyone wanted to trade for my peanut butter bars!

1 c. shortening
2 T. peanut butter
1 c. brown sugar

1 egg yolk
1 t. vanilla
2 c. flour

Cream together shortening, peanut butter and sugar until fluffy. Add egg yolk and vanilla, stir in flour. Spread in a well-greased 15"x11" jelly roll pan and bake at 350 degrees until light brown, about 20 to 30 minutes. Frost while hot.

Frosting:

1/2 c. peanut butter
4 to 6 T. milk

2 to 2-1/2 c. powdered sugar

Stir together frosting ingredients, adding more milk as needed to make it spreadable.

Banana Chocolate Chip Cookies *Michelle Stockton*
Billings, MT

*My favorite cookie because making them is a wonderful way
to spend the day with your family. This was one of the great
recipes my mom always made with us. Mom had many
wonderful recipes and passed them on to her kids. She's since
passed away, but her traditions live within us.*

1 stick margarine	2-1/4 c. flour
1 c. brown sugar	1 t. baking powder
2 eggs	1 t. baking soda
1 t. vanilla	12-oz. pkg. chocolate chips
3 bananas, mashed	

Mix all ingredients together in order listed and drop by
teaspoonfuls onto a greased cookie sheet. Bake at 375 degrees
for 8 to 10 minutes.

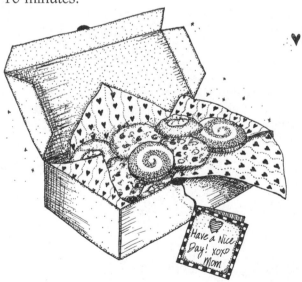

*Bananas that have already darkened can be peeled, frozen and placed
in a freezer container until you're ready use them in your favorite
bread or cake.*

Dutch Letters

Linda Routier
Grinnell, IA

A favorite tradition at our house! Every year we can count on Grandpa to say, "Whatever those things are, they're my favorite!" When I walk past the barber shop on my way to work, Marv the owner meets me at the door and robs a Dutch Letter from me. Now I just give him a plate full! I guess my husband has excellent taste, because he is the reason I'm still making these!

1 lb. shortening	2 c. sugar
4 c. flour	3 eggs
1 c. water	1 t. vanilla
1 lb. almond paste	egg white, beaten

Combine shortening, flour and water, mixing well, batter will be thin. Refrigerate over night, but no longer. Prepare filling by combining almond paste, sugar, eggs and vanilla mixing well; refrigerate overnight. When preparing to make cookies, divide dough and filling into 8 or 10 parts. Roll each piece of dough into a rectangle, spoon filling in center and roll lengthways. Firmly pinch ends to seal and brush tops with lightly beaten egg white. Using a fork, pierce tops of each roll. Bake at 400 degrees for 10 minutes.

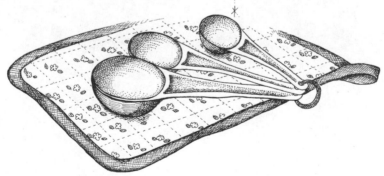

Test your eggs for freshness by placing them in a bowl or cup filled with water. If they float, it's time to replace them!

Homemade Root Beer

Mary Murray
Gooseberry Patch

Several years ago there was a church social held at our farm. It was a hot summer day, children were running everywhere and our picnic table was loaded with terrific potluck meals. A friend of ours made homemade root beer and served it in a milk can which kept it icy cold...it was wonderful! Better than anything you've ever tasted from the grocery store.

4 lbs. sugar
1 bottle root beer extract
5 gallons water

6 lbs. dry ice, broken in
　pieces

Mix sugar and extract together, then add water and dry ice. Let stand 20 minutes and serve icy cold. Makes 5 gallons.

Garnish fruit drinks with floating lemon or lime wedges, orange slices, or sprigs of fresh mint.

Cream Cheese Brownies

*Jean Landolfi
Northford, CT*

I have made these so many times I could bake them with my eyes closed! I'm asked to bring them whenever we have any kind of get-together. It wasn't handed down from my family, but it is being handed down to my children. My son said I <u>had</u> to send this recipe!

8-oz. pkg. cream cheese	2 c. flour
2-1/3 c. sugar	1 t. baking soda
3 eggs	1/2 t. salt
1 stick butter	1 t. vanilla
3/4 c. water	1/2 c. sour cream
2 oz. unsweetened chocolate, melted	1 c. chocolate chips

Combine cream cheese, 1/3 cup sugar and one egg; set aside. Mix butter, water and chocolate in a saucepan and heat until butter is melted. Mix together flour, remaining sugar, baking soda, salt, vanilla, eggs and sour cream. Blend into chocolate mixture. Spread into a greased and floured 17-1/2"x11" pan, spoon cream cheese mixture over chocolate mixture and marble with a knife. Sprinkle chocolate chips on top. Bake at 375 degrees for 25 to 30 minutes. Makes 32 brownies.

Chocolate easily picks up other flavors, so when you chill your cookie dough, beware of uncovered onions, garlic or other strong aromas in your refrigerator.

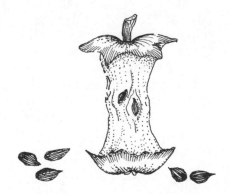

Peaches & Cream Cookies

Christi Miller
New Paris, PA

When I was 18 and a college student, I worked as a waitress in a little Italian restaurant for a wonderful family. They were always very good to me and treated me just like one of the family. I loved them with all my heart. My favorite was Speranza Neri, or Nana. She was the grandmother who founded the restaurant with her son. Nana was warm and beautiful and had lovely dark eyes that danced when she spoke of Italy and her younger days. When she left northern Italy to come to America, she was just 16. She was aboard the ship for several weeks and told of how many passengers became ill and how she helped to care for them. When she saw the Statue of Liberty she cried for joy! Her life-long dream had come true. This recipe is hers.

4 eggs
1 c. sugar
1 c. oil
4 c. flour
1 t. salt
1 t. vanilla
3 t. baking powder

1 lg. box instant vanilla
    pudding
12 oz. whipped topping
maraschino cherries
peach schnapps
peach-colored sugar

Mix eggs, sugar, oil, flour, salt, vanilla and baking powder, blending well; refrigerate overnight. Roll into small balls and bake at 350 degrees until very light brown, approximately 15 minutes. Combine pudding mix and whipped topping; set aside. Using 2 cookies for each "peach", take a small spoon and scoop out some cookie from the flat bottom. Fill both halves with the pudding mixture, place a maraschino cherry in the middle, for the peach pit, and put cookie halves back together. Brush the outside of each cookie with peach schnapps and roll in sugar. You can place a plastic or foil leaf in the top to complete your "peach".

Grandma's Finlanders

Laura Kitch
Superior, WI

I remember this recipe because their spicy aroma that reminds me of my grandma and Christmas. We only bake them once a year, during the Christmas season.

2 c. butter	2 t. ginger
2 c. brown sugar	2 t. cinnamon
4 eggs	2 t. orange peel
4 T. molasses	9 c. flour
1 c. cream	1/2 t. salt
1 t. cloves	2 t. baking soda
2 t. cardamom	

Cream butter and sugar; add eggs, molasses and cream. Sift dry ingredients together and add to liquid ingredients. Refrigerate overnight, roll very thin and cut into desired shapes. Bake at 350 degrees until lightly browned.

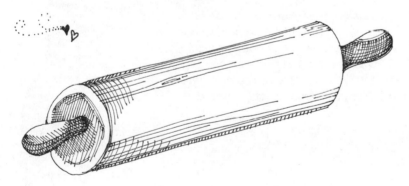

Do you know someone who needs a little lift? Fill a basket with books, a pretty teacup with teabags, home-grown flowers, candles, cookies, bubble bath and scented soaps. Tuck in some coupons for free babysitting, car wash or mowing the lawn.

Vin Brulé

Sherry Chaffin
Vicenza, Italy

Vin Brulé warms me all over during the winter. We are stationed in Vicenza, Italy and here it is a traditional Italian apértif.

1 bottle red table wine
pinch of nutmeg
pinch of cinnamon

pinch of cloves
1 lemon peel
1 c. sugar

Pour wine into a saucepan and bring to a boil. Add nutmeg, cinnamon, cloves and lemon peel. Add sugar in slowly to suit your taste. Best served in a clear mug with a stick of cinnamon. A great drink to share with friends during the holidays.

For a romantic wedding gift, fill a lace-lined hatbox with jars of your homemade jams, jellies, chocolates, a heart-shaped sachet, bottle of sparking cider and fluted glasses. Frame the wedding invitation and tuck in a pair of cut-glass candlesticks. Use doilies or a garter to decorate the tops of your jelly lids.

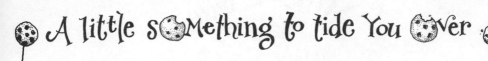

Carrot Cookies

LaWanda Gorton
Ottawa, KS

A favorite because of all the old memories it brings to mind and because of my dear, dear grandmother. She always had time for all 11 grandchildren. When we had teen-age parties she would come and make taffy for taffy pulls and she and Pop would join in the fun! Of all the things she cooked, her grand-children's favorite would be carrot cookies. No one would call them carrot cookies because carrots were good for you! We called them orange cookies. Now we have passed the tradition down to our grandchildren. They all love them, but of course they call them orange cookies!

1 c. shortening	2-1/2 c. flour
1 c. sugar	2-1/2 t. baking powder
1 egg	1 t. vanilla
1 c. carrots, cooked and mashed	1/4 t. salt

Beat shortening, sugar and egg together, add carrots. Add remaining ingredients and mix well. Cover and chill overnight. Drop by tablespoonfuls onto an ungreased cookie sheet. Bake at 350 degrees for 8 to 10 minutes. Cookies will be soft to the touch and lightly browned. Frost when removed from oven.

Orange Frosting:

1 box powdered sugar	1/4. butter
1 orange, juice and rind, grated	1 t. vanilla
	milk

Combine well, adding milk until of spreading consistency. Spread on cookies while still warm.

Cheesecake Cookies

Mary Walsh
Valencia, CA

These are my favorite cookies because they're so moist and tasty. I remember they were considered a special treat, usually made for company, but once in awhile, we'd come home from school and a pan of them warm from the oven would be waiting for us!

1/3 c. butter	8 oz. cream cheese
1/3 c. brown sugar	1 egg
1 c. flour	2 T. milk
1/2 c. walnuts, finely chopped	1 T. lemon juice
1/4 c. sugar	1/2 t. vanilla

Preheat oven to 350 degrees. Cream butter with brown sugar in a small mixing bowl. Add flour and walnuts. Mix together, mixture will be crumbly. Reserve one cup for topping. Press remainder of mixture into the bottom of an 8-inch square pan. Bake for 12 to15 minutes until lightly browned. Blend sugar with cream cheese until smooth. Add egg, milk, lemon juice and vanilla; beat well. Spread over baked crust and sprinkle with reserved topping. Bake for 25 minutes. Cool, cut into 2-inch squares.

On the last day of school send a plate of cookies to your child's teacher. It's a thoughtful gift that will leave good memories of the past year.

Summertime Iced Tea

Charlotte Harding
Starkville, MS

Refreshing on a hot summer day!

2 large teabags
6 fresh mint leaves
4 c. boiling water
1 c. sugar

6-oz. can frozen lemonade
   concentrate
5 c. water
fresh mint for garnish

Steep teabags and mint leaves for 5 minutes in boiling water. Discard teabags and mint. Add frozen lemonade, sugar and remaining water, mixing well. Serve over ice and garnish with fresh mint.

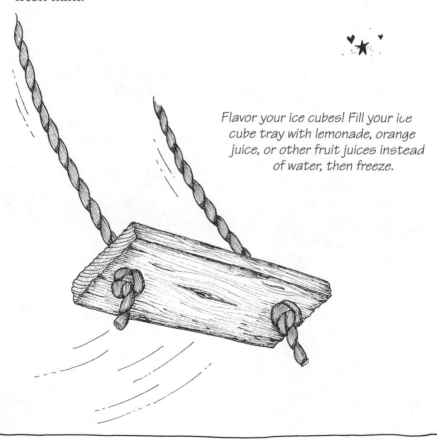

Flavor your ice cubes! Fill your ice cube tray with lemonade, orange juice, or other fruit juices instead of water, then freeze.

Oatmeal Cut-Outs

Melissa Gullion
Ottumwa, IA

These cookies have been such a long-standing tradition of Christmas for me and my family, I can't imagine not making them. I first got the recipe when I was 8 years old and playing at a friend's house. Her mother was baking and we were helping. They were so good and I had such a great time that I asked for the recipe. I've been making them for 25 years now! They're easy, delicious and an excellent recipe for cut-outs!

3/4 c. butter	1/2 t. baking soda
1/2 c. sugar	dash of salt
1/2 c. brown sugar	1-1/2 c. oatmeal
1 egg	powdered sugar for rolling
1 t. vanilla	dough on
1-2/3 c. flour	

Cream butter and sugars together. Add egg and vanilla and beat well. Blend in dry ingredients and chill overnight. Divide and roll on powdered sugar, cut with your favorite cookie cutters Bake at 350 degrees for 5 to 8 minutes. Makes approximately 3 dozen cookies, depending on the size of the cookie cutter.

Soda Fountain Concoctions

Carol Sheets
Gooseberry Patch

Years ago soda fountains were always found in drugstores. Many young children and teenagers saved their allowance to walk across the street to enjoy milkshakes, malts or Brown Cows!

Brown Cow

2 oz. evaporated milk
2 oz. chocolate syrup
crushed ice

root beer
chocolate sprinkles

Shake milk and syrup together, add ice and pour in a soda glass. Fill glass with root beer, top with sprinkles.

Malted Milk

2 scoops vanilla ice cream
2 oz. flavored syrup

milk
malted milk powder

Place ice cream and syrup in a tall glass or container with a lid, mix well. Add just enough milk to fill container, add malted milk powder, cover and shake until frothy.

Phosphates

2 t. sour salt
1 c. water

soda, your favorite type
1 scoop ice cream, any flavor

Dissolve sour salt (available in spice shops) in water; set aside. Fill a glass with soda, add ice cream and just a few drops of salt and water mixture.

June is National Dairy Month; celebrate by hosting an old-fashioned ice cream social!

Chocolate Fruitcake Cookies

Judy Hand
Centre Hall, PA

Having never liked fruitcake and feeling a tinge of guilt about my non-traditional stance to a very traditional Christmas confection, I was relieved when a friend gave me the following recipe. It is now my traditional "fruitcake offering" and gets thumbs up from those nay-sayers of fruitcake! It's a quick recipe that doesn't require baking.

1/2 lb. pecans, chopped
1/2 lb. raisins
1/2 lb. candied cherries
7-oz. can flaked coconut

1 box powdered sugar
2-3/4 c. graham crackers, crushed
1/2 lb. butter, melted

Mix pecans, raisins and cherries until well blended. Add coconut, sugar and graham crackers, mixing well. Add melted butter and shape into balls. Dip balls into chocolate coating.

Chocolate Coating:

1/2 lb. paraffin, melted

12 oz. chocolate chips

Melt paraffin and chips in top of a double boiler and use to coat cookies. After coating, dry on wax paper. Makes approximately 75 to 80 cookies.

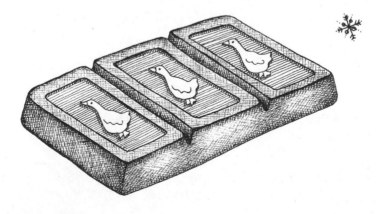

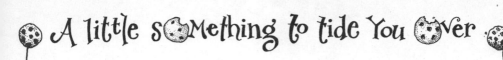

Summertime Watermelon Drink

Ana Huron
Tiger, GA

This drink provides the cooling refreshment of a slice of water-melon in a glass! It reminds my family of summer picnic days and breaks from harvesting and canning!

1 watermelon   1 to 2 cups of sugar

Slice and seed watermelon. Crush with a potato masher or clean hands (children love to help with this!) Add sugar and stir until dissolved. Using a ladle, scoop pulp into each glass. It also looks great in a punch bowl with cantaloupe or honey dew balls. Serves 10 to 20 depending on the size of the watermelon.

Calorie-free club soda adds sparkle to fruit juices without adding calories!

Montana Choco-Luckies

Deni Donich Corrigan
Anaconda, MT

I remember coming home from grade school and Mom would have a plate of these ready to dive into! For variety, experiment with different types of cake mixes; fudge, milk chocolate or mint-chocolate!

1/4 c. butter	1 egg, or 2 egg whites
6-oz. pkg. chocolate chips	1 pkg. chocolate cake mix
1/3 c. milk	1/2 c. walnuts, chopped

Combine butter and chocolate chips. Stir in milk and egg. Add cake mix and combine thoroughly, stir in walnuts. Drop by teaspoonfuls onto a lightly oiled cookie sheet. Bake at 350 for 10 minutes.

Dip your measuring cup in hot water before measuring butter; it will slip right out without sticking!

SUNDAY Dinner at GrandMa's

Please pass the chicken & dumplings

Honeymoon Chicken & Biscuits

Carol Blessing
Cropseyville, NY

When my husband and I were first married, his 80-year-old grandmother seemed less than convinced that I was deserving of so noble a gentleman…whenever she visited our home, she had lots of advice for me when it came to cooking and watched me like a hawk in the kitchen. Then one day I managed to make this dish while she was out on a ride with my husband. That night at dinner Grandma ate with wild abandon! By the time dinner was over there wasn't a trace of food left on her plate or in the bowl and Grandma was beginning to question if her grandson was deserving of so fine a cook! Grandma's 88 now and never fails to request this dish whenever she visits.

1 c. red onion, chopped
1/2 c. butter divided
1/4 c. dry sherry or water
10-1/2 oz. can chicken broth
1 c. all-purpose flour, divided
1 t. poultry seasoning
2-1/2 c. chicken breast,
    cooked and chopped

10 oz. fresh or frozen
    vegetables mushrooms,
    corn, carrots, peas, green
    beans
3/4 c. quick cooking oats
2 t. baking powder
1/2 c. skim milk
1 egg white
1 T. maple syrup

Cook onion in 2 tablespoons butter over medium-high heat for 3 minutes, or until tender. Add combined sherry, broth, 1/4 cup flour and seasoning. Cook an additional 3 minutes or until thick. Stir in chicken and vegetables and pour into a 2-quart casserole. Combine remaining flour, oats and baking powder. Cut in remaining butter until crumbly. Stir in milk, egg white and syrup until moist. Drop by 1/4 cupfuls onto chicken. Bake 35 to 42 minutes at 425 degrees. Serves 6 (unless Grandma's here!).

Biscuits can be dry if the dough is handled too much or if the oven temperature isn't hot enough.

Pot Roast & Gravy

Carol Welch
Savannah, GA

Leftovers are great for sandwiches!

1 t. garlic salt
1/2 t. onion powder
1/4 t. pepper
3 to 4 lb. roast
1/8 c. olive oil
1 large onion, chopped
1 small green pepper,
   chopped

2 cloves garlic, minced
2 bay leaves
1 t. parsley flakes
1/4 t. thyme
3/4 c. water
1/4 c. Worcestershire sauce
1/4 c. flour

Preheat oven to 325 degrees. Sprinkle or rub garlic salt, onion powder and pepper on roast, brown in oil; set aside. Combine onion, green pepper, garlic, bay leaves and parsley and sprinkle half in bottom of roasting pan. Add roast, and sprinkle remaining half of spices on meat. Combine thyme, water and Worcestershire sauce, pour over roast. Cover and cook slowly for 2 hours, turn roast, return to oven for another 2 hours or until roast is tender. To make gravy, remove enough drippings from roasting pan to equal 2 cups. Strain onion, green pepper and bay leaves from drippings and place in a skillet with flour. Stir until smooth and thick, salt and pepper to taste. Serves 6 to 8.

Add a few slices of tomato in with your roast. Tomatoes contain acid which will work to tenderize the meat naturally.

Mama's Sunday Pork Chops

Cyndy Sardeson
Ankeny, IA

The fanciest dish I knew how to make when I was a young bride. I remember it because I so enjoyed learning how to make it from my mother.

2 eggs, beaten
2 cracker sleeves
6 or 8 loin or butterfly pork
    chops, 1/2" to 3/4" thick
2 T. oil

2 10-3/4 oz. cans cream of
    mushroom soup
water
1/3 c. onion, finely chopped
salt and pepper to taste

In a medium bowl beat eggs and set aside. Put crackers in another bowl and crush. Dip pork chops in eggs then roll in cracker crumbs. Over medium heat, brown pork chops in oil for 10 minutes. Place pork chops in a 4 to 6-quart Dutch oven and spoon soup over top. Fill soup can 1/2 to 3/4 full of water and pour over soup mixture. sprinkle with chopped onion, salt and pepper to taste. Bake at 350 degrees for 1-1/2 hours. Makes 6 to 8 servings.

A quick and easy seasoning mix is six parts salt to one part pepper. Keep it handy in a large shaker close to the stove.

Aunt Ellen's Overnight Rolls

Jane Williams
Austin, MN

Aunt Ellen's rolls is one of my all-time favorite recipes! It suits my busy lifestyle and I can count on it to turn out wonderful homemade rolls time after time. Drizzle with some powdered sugar frosting…wonderful!

1 pkg. dry yeast	1 T. salt
1/4 c. warm water	2 eggs, beaten
3/4 c. butter, softened	6-1/2 c. flour
3/4 c. sugar	6 T. butter, divided
2 c. boiling water	9 T. cinnamon-sugar, divided
	1/2 c. almonds, slivered

Dissolve yeast in water and set aside. In a large bowl cream butter and sugar. Stir in boiling water; cool to lukewarm. Add salt, eggs and yeast mixture. Mix in flour. Cover with an oiled sheet of wax paper and place in refrigerator overnight. Divide dough into three sections and roll each into a 12"x9" rectangle. Spread each section with 2 tablespoons of butter, sprinkle with 3 tablespoons cinnamon-sugar. Roll each jelly-roll style; pinching ends to seal. Slice each roll into 12 equal portions and place in greased muffin tins. Allow to rise one hour then bake at 350 degrees for 15 minutes. This recipe can also be converted to make coffee cakes. Prepare recipe as above, but instead of slicing, flatten each roll into a width of 4 inches. Slash tops 6 to 8 times and allow to rise one hour. Bake at 350 degrees for 20 minutes. Frost and sprinkle with almonds. Makes 3 dozen rolls or 3 coffee cakes.

Granny's Chicken & Dumplings

Robin Wilson
Altamonte Springs, FL

My grandmother is very special to our family. For as long as I can remember she made this recipe for family and church gatherings. The former pastor of her church always expected her to bring this dish!

1 chicken	1 t. salt
3 c. all-purpose flour	1 egg

Cut chicken into pieces and thoroughly rinse with water. Place in a large stockpot and cover with water. Cook 1-1/2 to 2 hours, or until tender. Add salt and pepper to taste. After chicken has cooked one hour, remove 3/4 cup of broth and let cool. While chicken continues to cook, place flour and salt in a mixing bowl, making a well in the center. Add egg and cooled broth. Mix in flour until a soft dough is formed. Place dough on a pastry sheet sprinkled with flour and roll until thin. Cut into 1"x2" strips and let stand 15 minutes. When chicken is done, remove from broth, skin and debone. Bring broth to a rolling boil; drop dumplings in one at a time. Add chicken and cook uncovered for an additional 10 to 15 minutes.

How dear to this heart are the scenes of my childhood, when fond recollection presents them to view.

-Samuel Woodworth

Peppered Roast

Elaine Corcovilos
Ravenswood, WV

A versatile dish that can be served for every-day or saved for special occasions.

2 t. cracked pepper
2 t. dry mustard
1/2 t. ground allspice
1/2 t. ground red pepper

1 large clove garlic, minced
1 t. oil
3-1/2 to 5 lb. eye of round
  roast

Mix spices with oil and rub over roast on all sides. Insert meat thermometer in the thickest part of the roast. Place uncovered in a 325 degree oven until thermometer reaches 140 degrees for medium-rare or 155 degrees for medium; approximately 30 to 35 minutes per pound. Let stand 15 minutes before carving.

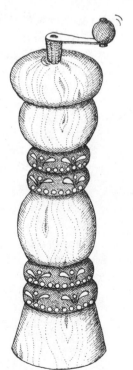

Marinating is easy when you use a plastic locking bag. The meat is sealed in with the marinade and all you do is turn the bag to coat the meat. Clean up's a breeze!

Mom's Baked Spaghetti

Kim Henry
Library, PA

This recipe was given to me by my mother-in-law and has been in the family for years. Whenever I bake this, people are always requesting the recipe. It can be made the night before and placed in the refrigerator and cooked the next day. Serve with garlic bread and salad.

1 lb. spaghetti
2 T. butter
8 oz. Old English cheese slices
8 oz. American cheese slices
2 8-oz. cans tomato sauce

Italian seasoning
8-oz. can grated Parmesan cheese
1 lb. can crushed tomatoes
sugar
salt and pepper

Cook spaghetti according to package directions and drain. Stir in butter until melted and mixed through spaghetti. Put one-third of spaghetti in a large buttered casserole or deep baking dish. Top with dots of butter and sprinkle with salt and pepper. Cover spaghetti with broken pieces of cheese. Pour tomato sauce on cheese, sprinkle with Italian seasoning and Parmesan cheese. Repeat layers two more times, end with crushed tomatoes on top. Sprinkle with sugar, salt and pepper, top with more Parmesan. Bake at 350 degrees for one hour or until top is golden and edges are bubbly. Cool for 10 minutes before serving. Serves 6 to 8.

For a thoughtful hostess gift, give a jar of pesto sauce and a potted basil plant in a grapevine basket tied with a raffia bow.

Cheesy Garlic Biscuits

Teri Lindquist
Gurnee, IL

Perfect with any meal and so delicious! There are never any leftovers at my house!

2 c. biscuit mix
2/3 c. milk
1/2 c. Cheddar cheese,
   shredded

1/4 c. butter, melted
1/2 t. garlic powder

Preheat oven to 450 degrees. Mix together biscuit mix, milk and cheese until a soft dough forms. Shape into balls and arrange on a greased cookie sheet. Bake 10 minutes, or until golden, watching carefully. Combine butter and garlic powder. Brush over each biscuit as soon as they are removed from the oven.

In a hurry to cut your biscuits? Use a metal ice tray divider!

Pork Roast & Sauerkraut

*Paula James
Edgar Springs, MO*

Absolutely delicious! Not too sweet or tart and very filling. When I was a child, this was the recipe my mom made on really cold days. I can remember being out of school because of snow, and spending the day outside making snow angels and sledding. Mom would call me inside for dinner and there would be a hot plate of pork roast to warm me up.

pork roast	2 tart apples, peeled, cored
2 T. oil	and sliced
2 cans sauerkraut	4 to 6 potatoes, peeled and
1/4 c. brown sugar	quartered

Brown pork roast in oil and put in a roaster. Add remaining ingredients and bake at 350 degrees for 2 to 2-1/2 hours or until thoroughly cooked.

The kitchen is the heart of every home beckoning with warmth and hospitality. Decorate your kitchen with homey touches and simple things...baskets of red wooden apples, bowls of potpourri, fragrant garlands and warm, inviting colors.

Marinated Brisket

Neta Jo Liebscher
El Reno, OK

I like to put my brisket on early Sunday morning so it will be ready for a house-full of family after church. Growing up on a farm, my children were spoiled with home-grown beef, and brisket was their favorite. Now that our children are grown, my husband and I look forward to the Sundays when they, and their families, come home for their favorite Mom-cooked meal.

2 T. liquid smoke	4 to 5 lb. brisket
1 T. Worcestershire sauce	3 T. brown sugar
4 T. soy sauce	1/2 c. catsup
2 t. salt	1 t. dry mustard
2 t. onion salt	3 drops hot sauce
2 t. garlic salt	1 t. lemon juice
2 t. pepper	1 T. soy sauce
1 T. celery salt	dash of nutmeg

Mix first 8 ingredients in order and marinate brisket overnight or longer, turning every few hours. Remove from marinade and bake at 300 degrees for 3-1/2 hours. Mix remaining ingredients and top roast for the last 45 minutes of cooking.

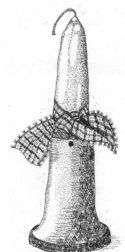

Never cook a roast cold! Let it stand for at least an hour at room temperature and brush with oil to help seal in the juices.

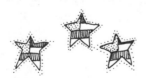

Sunday Milk Chicken

Sandra Matthijetz
Winchester, TX

In 1938 when my parents married, they first lived with my Dad's parents and his two brothers. They shared a two-room house without electricity or running water. My mother always remarked how resourceful my grandmother was to feed 6 adults with whatever she happened to have on hand. There were always chickens in the pen and plenty of milk from Betsy. This has become a family favorite and we always remember her when we cook it today. Grandma served this with new potatoes, fresh greens and thick slices of homemade bread.

1 frying chicken	margarine
salt and pepper to taste	1 onion, chopped
flour, enough to coat chicken	milk

Cut rinsed chicken into pieces, place in a stockpot and cover with water, boil until done. Remove chicken from broth; salt, pepper and coat with flour. In a skillet, melt margarine, add onion and chicken. Brown chicken on all sides then gradually add milk until chicken is nearly covered. Cover and simmer until milk gravy develops.

Pictures of loved ones remind us of precious ties to our past. Decorate a double heart frame with eyelet and ribbon, insert a favorite family picture.

Mom's Dressing

Belinda Gibson
Amarillo, TX

Every Thanksgiving and Christmas my mom always cooked a huge turkey and her wonderful dressing. One Christmas my older brother was holding the turkey in the pan to pour the turkey juice into the dressing mix. His hand slipped and the turkey flew out of the pan and skidded across the kitchen floor! Mom was shocked when all four kids started laughing and told her we didn't care about the turkey, we all wanted the dressing! Now we tease Mom every year, please cook a smaller turkey and make two pans of dressing! This recipe came from my grandmother.

1 large pan cornbread crumbled, your favorite recipe
10 slices stale bread, torn
2 sticks butter
4 eggs

1 small onion, chopped
salt, pepper, celery salt to
   taste
sage to taste, crumbled

Combine all ingredients together in a large bowl. Add juices from cooked turkey until mixture is soupy. Toss gently, bake covered for 1-1/2 hours at 350 degrees.

Foods that have burned on the stove are easy to remove. Apply baking soda to the spots, rub with a damp cloth and rinse with clear water.

My Husband's Meatloaf *Barry and Audra Webb*
Halifax, VA

This is a recipe that's very dear to me. It's not fancy food or some new chic style of eating, but it's dear to me because it was the first meal my husband ever truly prepared for mere surprise. He put a lot of time and effort into making it. I was very touched by his effort...and it tasted great too!

1 lb. hamburger	1 T. catsup
1 egg	dash of Worcestershire sauce
1/2 sleeve saltine crackers	salt and pepper to taste
1 pkg. onion-mushroom dry soup mix	

Mix all ingredients thoroughly, shape into a loaf and place in a microwaveable dish. Cook in microwave on low for 15 to 20 minutes. Drain excess liquids and top with sauce.

Sauce:

10-3/4 oz. can tomato soup   1/2 c. water
1/2 c. brown sugar

Put all ingredients into a saucepan and mix over low heat until thoroughly warmed. Pour over meatloaf. Serves 4.

Your meatloaf won't stick to the loaf pan if you place a slice of bacon in the bottom and place the meatloaf on top.

Easy Macaroni & Cheese

Marilyn Hall
Vancouver, WA

This recipe from my sister-in-law is a favorite because it's so easy and delicious!

2 c. macaroni, uncooked
2 c. milk
2 c. Cheddar cheese, cubed

10-3/4 oz. can cream of
   mushroom soup
1/4 onion, chopped

Preheat oven to 350 degrees. Combine all ingredients in a casserole dish. Bake one hour, uncovered, stirring once during baking. Serves 4 to 6.

Pull out Grandma's button box and create some clever country napkin rings. Using a 4-inch length of heavy-weight cord elastic, thread on buttons and tie off ends with a knot. Pretty when stretched around a napkin made from calico or homespun.

Ham, Peas & Potato Casserole

Connie Walker
Hebron, MD

This makes a great home-cooked, warm dinner. It's great to make for friends who have just come home with a new baby...just pack it up with a fresh loaf of bread, the fixin's for a salad and dinner's all ready!

1 c. celery, chopped
1/2 t. salt
1-1/2 c. boiling water
1-1/2 c. cubed potatoes
milk
1/4 c. butter
1/4 c. onion, chopped

1/4 c. flour
2 c. ham, cubed
2 T. parsley, chopped
1 c. cooked peas
1/2 c. your favorite cheese, grated

Add celery and salt to boiling water, cook for 10 minutes. Add potatoes and cook 15 minutes longer, drain and reserve liquid. Add enough milk to potato water to equal 1-1/2 cups liquid. In a large saucepan, melt butter, add onion and cook over low heat until tender. Add flour and blend well, gradually adding liquid, stirring until sauce thickens. Boil for one minute and remove from heat. Add ham, parsley, celery, potatoes and peas. Spoon into an oiled 1-1/2 quart casserole dish and top with cheese. Bake, uncovered, at 325 degrees for 30 minutes or until hot and bubbly. You can also make this casserole a day in advance and refrigerate overnight, just bake at 350 degrees for 45 minutes.

Fill wide-mouth canning jars with special treats for a friend...mini chocolate chip cookies, embroidery floss, flower bulbs, or buttons. Cross stitch a design on a square of fabric large enough to cover the jar lid. Glue batting on top of lid, glue cross-stitch design to batting and glue lid inside screw ring.

Mandarin Orange Salad

Laura Townsend
Redding, CA

I remember my great-grandmother, who immigrated from Australia, whenever I make this salad. It's summer in Australia at Christmas time so she always made this light dish to go along with the traditional heavy English Christmas meal.

3 cans mandarin oranges, sliced
1 envelope unflavored gelatin
2 3-oz. pkgs. orange gelatin

12-oz. can frozen orange juice
16 oz. sour cream

Drain mandarin oranges, reserving juice. Pour juice in a measuring cup, adding enough water to make 2-1/2 cups of liquid. Bring liquid to a boil and add gelatins. Stir in orange juice and cool to room temperature. Add sour cream, mix thoroughly and fold in orange slices. Pour into an 11"x7" rectangular pan and refrigerate until set.

To keep from washing and wiping measuring cups and spoons repeatedly, use two sets of untensils to measure ingredients.

Hobo Packs

Peg Ackerman
Pasadena, CA

One of the first things I ever cooked was a Hobo Pack at Brownie Day Camp. What memories they bring back! When I was a Scout Leader, we made these for one of our cookouts. Everyone got to put theirs together assembly-line style. While the packs were on the coals, we played games and sang songs. This is a favorite because the fun is in the results as well as the preparation and eating! There was very little to clean up after dinner because we ate right out of the foil.

1 hamburger pattie	2 carrots, sliced
1 slice onion	salt and pepper
1 small potato, sliced in half	

Prepare a bed of charcoal and ignite. On a large piece of heavy foil, shiny side up, center the hamburger pattie and layer the remaining ingredients, sprinkle with salt and pepper. Bring up sides of foil and fold over to seal. When coals are hot, place Hobo Packs on foil and cook 30 to 35 minutes, turning 3 or 4 times during the cooking time. Serve with French bread or rolls and eat right out of the foil.

To make easy s'mores, wrap up your ingredients in a square of aluminum foil, seal the edges well. Toss on the outer edges your bonfire and let sit 5 minutes or until chocolate and marshmallows have melted! Unwrap and enjoy!

Cowboy Food

Dixie K. Barkley
Hope Hull, AL

This is now being enjoyed by three generations of Barkleys, their friends and extended families. I first came upon this recipe in a newspaper years ago. The woman who submitted it said it looked like what cowboys had on their plates in all the old western movies, hence the name, Cowboy Food. This recipe can be doubled or tripled, and I always get requests for the recipe. Another indication of its importance is the first call that comes from a new daughter-in-law asking, "How do you make Cowboy Food?"

1 lb. ground beef
1 can Spanish rice
1 can chili beans

1 to 2 c. Cheddar cheese, shredded

Brown the ground beef in a large skillet and drain. Add rice and beans and return to heat until bubbly. Stir in cheese and allow to melt. You can also combine all ingredients in a casserole dish and bake at 350 degrees for 30 minutes. Great served with garlic bread and a salad.

Divide your bread dough into smaller portions and bake in a prepared tin can. When cool, tie a bandanna around the top of the can for a western accent!

Mother's Roasted Chicken

Dee Fitzpatrick
Dumont, NJ

Roast chicken is so easy to prepare and smells delicious while it's roasting!

3 lb. chicken	1/2 t. onion powder
2 t. salt	1/2 t. thyme
1 t. paprika	1/4 t. garlic powder
3/4 t. pepper	1 c. onion, chopped

Thoroughly rinse inside and out of chicken. Combine seasonings and rub on outside of chicken. Place chicken in a plastic bag, refrigerate overnight. Before roasting, stuff the cavity with chopped onion and roast uncovered at 250 degrees for 5 hours.

Freeze summer corn to enjoy this winter. Place unhusked ears of corn in a brown grocery bag, roll down and secure the top with a rubber band, place the bags on a shelf in your freezer. When ready to use, let corn thaw enough to husk and prepare in boiling water as you normally would.

Nanny's Holiday Dressing

Annie Wolfe
Gooseberry Patch

One of my favorite times of the year is Thanksgiving. When I was younger, my mom always made the best pies and desserts, but what I loved the best was her homemade dressing for turkey. I remember the love and fun that went into making it. On Thanksgiving morning we always turned on the television to watch the Macy's Day Parade. My brother Norman and I would sit on the living room floor breaking loaves of bread into bite-size pieces and, when the pan was filled, Mom would add the rest of her ingredients. Since we were a military family, Mom and Dad would open up their hearts and home to all the young airmen who would have otherwise been alone. Now my family follows the same tradition that Mom started so many years ago. As we make the dressing, I feel that Mom is right there with us.

4 loaves wheat bread	1/2 to 3/4 c. walnuts, chopped
2 loaves white bread	
1 c. onions, chopped	turkey or chicken broth
1/2 to 1 cup celery, chopped	salt and pepper to taste
1 stick butter	poultry seasoning to taste

Tear bread into bite-size pieces; set aside. Sauté onions and celery in butter while heating broth in a large saucepan. Add sautéed onions, celery and nuts to the broken bread. Cut butter into 4 slices, add to bread mixture, and pour in enough broth to moisten bread. Use a potato masher to mix ingredients. Add salt, pepper and poultry seasoning to taste. When thoroughly combined, spoon into a 13"x9" casserole dish and pour an additional 1/2 to 3/4 cups of broth over top of dressing to keep it moist. Bake at 375 degrees for 20 to 25 minutes. Makes 10 to 12 servings.

...just like mom used to make!

Beef Stroganoff

Susan Bowman
Moline, IL

This recipe is from my mom who was a working mom in the '60's and '70's when I grew up; however she always had time to serve us a hot meal at night. Now, as a working mom in the '90's, I can only try to follow in my mom's footsteps and recipes like this help.

1-1/2 to 2 lbs. stew meat
2 T. flour
1 large onion, chopped
4-oz. jar mushrooms, sliced
2 T. oil

1 can beef broth
1/4 c. sherry
1 T. dry mustard
1 c. sour cream
salt and pepper to taste

Dredge meat in flour and set aside, then sauté onions and mushrooms in oil. Remove from skillet, brown meat on both sides and return onions and mushrooms to skillet. Add broth, sherry and mustard and simmer until meat is tender, approximately one hour. Add sour cream and simmer 10 to 15 minutes more. Serve over rice or noodles.

Share your homemade goodies with a friend. Tuck a jar of bread-and-butter pickles or apple pie filling in a spray-painted fruit basket. Tie a long strip of homespun in a bow around the top and bottom of the basket.

Gram's Polish Soup Noodles

Betty Richer
Grand Junction, CO

These noodles are hearty and the best-ever noodles! I remember walking into her house, smelling the chicken soup and hearing Dad ask, "Homemade noodles too, Ma?", a "yes" from Gram and that smile from Dad! Take the time to enjoy some of the past. It's worth the extra effort.

3 eggs, well beaten	1-3/4 c. flour
3/4 c. water, luke warm	

Mix all ingredients until a dough forms. Roll on a well-floured board until thin. Dry for 1/2 hour, then cut into strips. Fill a 3-quart saucepan half full of water and cook until tender, about 20 minutes. Add to your favorite soup recipe. Enough for a large pot of soup.

Grandma's old tea kettle makes the perfect vase for a pretty pot of daisies.

Stuffed Cabbage Rolls

Lisa Ekstrom
Kentland, IN

Known as Golabki, this is my favorite Polish recipe because it is tasty, easy to prepare, and a dish my grandmother handed down to her daughters-in-law to prepare for her sons. I've done my best to continue this tasty tradition.

1 head cabbage
1 c. rice, long-cooking
1/2 t. salt
1-1/2 to 2 lbs. ground beef
1 medium onion
2 eggs

garlic salt, parsley, celery
   seed, pepper and
   oregano to taste
1 T. Worcestershire sauce
1 jar spaghetti sauce

Cut core from cabbage and boil in a large pot of water until leaves separate; blot dry. Boil rice in 2 cups of water with salt for 2 minutes. Turn off heat and allow to cool. Mix beef, onion, eggs and seasonings together. Spoon into individual cabbage leaves and roll, tucking ends under. Put cabbage rolls in a roaster or large baking pan. Cover with sauce and bake covered for 1-1/2 hours at 350 degrees.

All too soon our little ones will be grown. Capture their bubbly smiles and first steps in a fabric-covered photo album. Cover the album in soft-colored flannel, decorate it with eyelet, ribbon or lace. Embroider baby's name and birthdate on the cover.

Ham Logs

Kathryn Poovey
Oxford, KS

A family favorite from young to old at our house! We serve it with sweet potatoes and apples. A wonderful aroma!

1/2 lb. ground ham
1/2 lb. pork sausage
1/4 c. dry bread crumbs
1 egg, beaten
1/3 c. milk

1/3 c. brown sugar
2 T. vinegar
2 T. water
1/4 t. dry mustard

Combine ham, sausage, bread crumbs, egg and milk and shape into 8 logs approximately 3 inches long. Place in a baking dish while preparing glaze. In a saucepan combine brown sugar, vinegar, water and dry mustard and boil for 2 minutes. Pour half of glaze over ham logs and bake at 350 degrees for 25 to 30 minutes. Add remaining glaze and bake 20 minutes longer, or until golden brown.

Make crumbs by placing crackers in a heavy-duty plastic zip-top bag and roll with a rolling pin or pound with a meat mallet. So easy and no mess!

Pork Loin & Potatoes

Patricia Murdick
Three Rivers, MI

 Simply tastes great!

1 T. olive oil
1 T. butter
4-1/2 inch thick pork loin
   or rib chops
4 medium-sized potatoes,
   peeled, cut into 1/4-inch
   lengths
1 medium onion, sliced

1/2 t. salt
1/8 t. pepper
2 t. lemon juice
1 t. oregano
1 green pepper, cored and
   quartered
1 tomato, cut into wedges

Heat oil and butter in a 10-inch skillet over medium heat. Brown pork loin or chops on both sides. Arrange potatoes and onion in skillet, sprinkle with salt, pepper, lemon juice and oregano. Cook over low heat for 30 minutes, stirring occasionally. Add green pepper and cook for 5 additional minutes, garnish with tomato wedges. Serves 4.

Stay, stay at home,
my heart and rest;
home-keeping
hearts are
happiest.

-Henry
Wadsworth
Longfellow

Cornbread Dressing

Barbara Poole
Macon, GA

When I was growing up, there were five kids in our family and there wasn't a lot of money for extras…until Christmas. Somehow Mama and Daddy managed to make magic happen every December 25th. Thanks to Mama's wonderful cooking and Daddy's moonlighting, we always had a chicken and Mama's special cornbread dressing! This is a bred-to-the-bone Southern recipe! Mama was born in Tennessee and now lives in Louisiana.

2 large onions	3 green onions, chopped
1 hen	1 stick butter
4 ribs of celery, chopped	1 T. poultry seasoning
2 slices of bread	salt and pepper to taste
1 large pan cornbread	5 eggs, beaten

Quarter one onion and boil with hen and one rib of celery. Continue to boil until meat is easily removed from the bone. Remove meat and reserve broth. Chop remaining onion and combine with crumbled breads, green onion and remaining celery in a large mixing bowl; set aside. Heat 3 to 4 cups of broth in a saucepan; add butter and bring to a boil. Pour broth over bread and cornbread; mix well. Bread mixture should appear soupy, add more broth if too dry. Add seasonings to taste and eggs. Place reserved meat in an oiled 13"x9" pan and pour dressing mixture on top. Bake at 350 degrees for one hour, or until golden brown. Serves 10 to 12.

Garlic-Lemon Chicken

Amy Herbert
Aurora, IL

Guests are so surprised by the flavor of this ordinary-looking dish. Very juicy and the marinade flavors can be tasted in every bite. Great served with a green salad and roasted potatoes, carrots and onions.

8 cloves garlic, peeled and
    chopped
2 t. salt
5 large lemons
2 t. paprika

3 t. black pepper
3/4 c. olive oil
8 boneless, skinless chicken
    breasts

Combine garlic and salt in a large bowl or locking plastic bag, allow to sit 5 minutes. Juice lemons and add to garlic and salt. Mix in paprika, pepper and olive oil. Whisk all ingredients well, or shake bag, add chicken and coat well. Marinate at least 12 hours, but no longer than 24 hours. Remove chicken from marinade, don't drain. Grill chicken over medium-high heat, turning often, for 22 to 25 minutes, or bake in an oven at 350 degrees for 40 to 45 minutes, or until juices run clear, turning once. Serves 8.

To increase the amount of juice you'll get when you squeeze a lemon, microwave the whole lemon on high power for 20 to 30 seconds before cutting and squeezing.

Cheese-Filled Ravioli

Lisa Bakos
Stephens City, VA

This brings back so many childhood sights, sounds, tastes and smells!

1 lb. ricotta	salt and pepper to taste
1 egg	3 c. flour
fresh parsley, minced	5 eggs
1/2 to 3/4 c. grated Romano	1/2 egg shell of water

Mix first 5 ingredients for filling and set aside. Prepare dough by placing flour in a large bowl and making a well in the center. Fill well with eggs, beat mixture with a fork. When eggs are thoroughly mixed, add water as needed to make a dough. Divide dough into two balls. Roll out onto a floured board and cut into squares with a knife or pizza cutter. Fill with one tablespoon of filling, fold over and press ends together with a floured fork. Boil 15 minutes and serve with marinara sauce and freshly grated cheese. Serves 6.

Having family and friends over for a New Year's dinner? Decorate your table with clocks of every size and shape, add candles and sprinkle confetti on the table. Create a festive spirit!

Mom's Chicken Pot Pie

Denise Rounds
Tulsa, OK

A good old-fashioned flavor, although I don't know why this is called a pot pie...it's not a pot pie at all, but has had this name for three generations, and I'm not going to argue with that! As I grew up, we had dinner at my grandmother's home and we always had this special dinner. Grandmother learned it from her mother-in-law so she could please my grandfather. He was working in the oil fields of Oklahoma in the early years of their marriage and came home really hungry! Grandma served this with succotash, hot dinner rolls and baked apples for dessert. Since she died, I've learned to make this recipe. It holds a very warm place in my memory and I'm passing it on to my children too. Wonderful on a cold winter night!

1 chicken, washed and
   rinsed
3 c. water
1 carrot, sliced
2 ribs celery with leaves,
   sliced

1 small onion, sliced
4 c. all-purpose flour
1 t. salt
2 T. shortening
1-1/2 c. cold water

Place chicken in a large stockpot with water, carrot, celery and onion. Simmer uncovered until the chicken is tender, approximately 2 hours. Remove chicken and strain vegetables from stock. Return stockpot to stove over medium-high heat. Set chicken on a platter in a warm oven. Combine flour, salt and shortening together, mixing by hand. Add water, a little at a time until flour mixture is moist. Divide mixture into two sections and roll out thinly on a floured surface. Cut dough into 2-inch squares and drop them one at a time into the boiling stock. Boil uncovered for 15 to 20 minutes, adding a little flour to the broth to thicken it. When ready to serve, combine broth mixture and chicken. Serves 4 to 6.

French Beef Dip

Donna Ford
Longview, TX

A favorite because everyone who has ever eaten it, loved it! We have taken it to the beach as well as enjoyed it in the winter.

3 to 4 lb. roast   1 pkg. onion soup mix
2 T. yellow mustard

Place meat in a slow cooker, cover with mustard then sprinkle onion soup mix on top. Cover and cook on low for 10 to 12 hours, or on high for 5 to 6 hours. When fully cooked, carve into thick slices or shred. Serve with vegetables or as a sandwich. Strain broth and skim fat. Dip or pour juice on French rolls, add mustard and meat. Messy, but delicious!

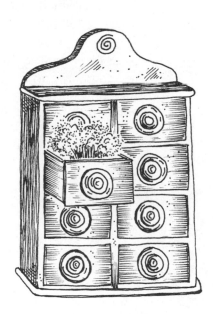

Enjoy more time with your family by using your slow-cooker; it does all the cooking for you!

Artichoke & Tomato Casserole

Molly Bordonaro
Worthington, OH

My mother has prepared this casserole for all important family events ever since I can remember. We always give it a place of honor at our Thanksgiving table, and it never fails to provoke the excited comment, "Oh, boy! Mom's bringing her artichoke casserole!" We always beg her to make it, and no matter how much she makes, there's never enough. That's because, in the rare instances where there might be a little dab of leftovers, my sister Nicky sneaks into the fridge in the middle of the night and eats it cold, right out of the pan.

2 c. plain bread crumbs
1/2 c. olive oil
3/4 c. Romano cheese, grated
garlic powder to taste

salt and pepper to taste
3 16-oz. pkgs. frozen artichoke hearts, sliced
28-oz. can peeled tomatoes, chopped and drained

Mix bread crumbs, oil, cheese and seasonings. Grease a large casserole dish; layer artichokes, tomatoes and crumb mixture in the dish, ending up with crumbs on the top. Drizzle a little water and olive oil on top, just enough to moisten. Cover and bake for 30 minutes at 350 degrees. Remove lid and continue to bake 10 to 15 minutes longer, until crumbs are brown. Test with knife for doneness. Serves 8.

If you're taking a casserole to a potluck or picnic, keep it hot by covering the casserole dish with foil then wrapping it in several layers of newspaper.

Shrimp & Wild Rice

Teresa Mulhern
Powell, OH

I've used this many times for potlucks and never have to bring home leftovers! It's also a great main dish served with salad and bread!

3/4 lb. shrimp, peeled and cleaned
1 box long grain and wild rice mix (not fast-cooking)
1/3 c. white rice, uncooked
1 medium yellow onion, chopped
1 medium green pepper, chopped

1 stick butter
8 oz. mushrooms, washed and sliced
salt and pepper to taste
2 shakes hot pepper sauce
1 c. heavy cream
1/4 c. almonds, slivered or sliced

Cook and clean shrimp; set aside. Prepare wild rice mix according to package directions. Add white rice, but no additional water when preparing. Sauté onion and green pepper in butter until tender, add mushrooms and seasonings. Remove from heat, add cream, rice mixture and allow to cool slightly. Add shrimp mixing well and pour into a buttered casserole dish, top with almonds. Bake at 350 degrees for 30 minutes, uncovered.

Spaghetti Sauce & Meatballs

Laurie Eckerty
Paxton, IL

My favorite recipe because it's better than any dish I've tasted in an Italian restaurant.

Sauce:

3/4 c. onion
1 clove garlic, minced
3 T. olive oil
1 lb. canned tomatoes,
   drained
2 6-oz. cans tomato paste

1 c. water
1 T. sugar
1-1/2 t. salt
1/2 t. pepper
1-1/2 t. crushed oregano
1 bay leaf

Cook onion and garlic in oil until tender. Stir in remaining ingredients and simmer uncovered for 30 minutes. Remove bay leaf, add meatballs and continue cooking for 30 minutes over low heat.

Meatballs:

4 slices slightly dry bread
1 lb. ground chuck
2 eggs
1/2 c. Romano, grated
2 T. parsley, chopped

1 clove garlic, minced
1 t. crushed oregano
1 t. salt
dash of pepper
2 T. corn oil

Soak bread in water for 2 to 3 minutes and squeeze moisture out. Combine bread with remaining ingredients and mix well. Form into small balls and brown slowly in oil. Add to sauce.

Need a quick, last-minute dessert? Slice peaches in a clear glass trifle dish, add fresh blueberries and sprinkle with sugar. Garnish with mint leaves before serving.

Pretzel Salad

Stephanie Ortner
Whittier, CA

My mother serves Pretzel Salad on special occasions such as birthdays and Christmas. Everyone always asks for a second helping!

Crust:

2 c. pretzels, crushed
3/4 c. butter, melted

3 T. sugar

Mix crust ingredients together and spread in a 13"x9" baking pan. Bake at 350 degrees for 10 minutes. Cool.

Filling:

8 oz. cream cheese, softened
1 c. sugar

8 oz. frozen whipped topping, thawed

Combine filling ingredients and spread evenly over crust.

Topping:

2 3-oz. pkgs. strawberry gelatin

2 c. boiling water
2 pkgs. frozen strawberries

Dissolve gelatin in boiling water. Drain juice from strawberries and mix with gelatin mixture. Add strawberries and allow to firm slightly before spreading over filling.

Take time for all things.

-Benjamin Franklin

Chicken Surprise

Dianna Runyan
Delaware, OH

Everyone always wants this recipe, there are never any leftovers!

7 or 8 chicken breast halves
1 box butter crackers, crushed
1 stick butter, melted
10-3/4 oz. can cream of chicken soup
10-3/4 oz. can cream of celery soup
1 can water chestnuts, sliced
1 onion, chopped
16 oz. sour cream

Cook chicken and shred. Combine crackers with melted butter, reserve one cup for topping. Pat remaining cracker crumbs into a 13"x9" baking dish. Combine chicken, soups, water chestnuts, onion and sour cream and spread evenly over crust. Sprinkle reserved crumbs over top. Cover and bake 30 minutes at 350 degrees, uncover bake 5 to 10 minutes longer.

When making croutons, use a pizza cutter to slice through the bread… it's faster than a knife.

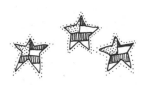

Winter Cabbage Stew

Janet Bordonaro
Fairborn, OH

*When it comes to "comfort foods," this is at the top of my
list...especially on cold winter days. The sausage makes a
flavorful broth; I like to add lots of extra pepper. Delicious with
buttered and broiled slices of crusty French bread; keep the
strawberry jam handy.*

2 lbs. smoked link sausage
6 medium potatoes, peeled
   and chopped
1 medium head cabbage,
   chopped

salt and pepper to taste
1 t. celery seed

Cut sausage into 2-inch lengths. Put in a large soup pot with 3
cups of water. Cover, bring to a slow simmer and cook over low
heat 15 minutes. Add potatoes, another cup of water and
seasonings. Cook uncovered an additional 15 minutes. Add
cabbage and 2 more cups of water. Cover and simmer until
cabbage is tender, about 15 minutes longer. Add additional salt
and pepper to taste. Serves 6 to 8.

*Making a casserole for a small family? Divide the casserole
ingredients into two small dishes and freeze one for later. Casseroles
that don't freeze well can be shared with a friend or neighbor.*

Bullfrog Mountain Special

Liz Kenneweg
Gooseberry Patch

This is an easy dish I make when my husband and I spend time at our rustic cabin hide-away. Serve it with a loaf of bread and a tossed salad.

1 onion, diced
1-1/2 lb. ground beef
2 32-oz. cans pork and
   beans
1/2 to 3/4 c. brown sugar

1/4 to 1/2 c. catsup
1/2 t. mustard
1/2 t. Worcestershire
8 to 10 slices your favorite
   type cheese

In a large skillet sauté onions and ground beef, drain. In another skillet combine beans, brown sugar, catsup, mustard and Worcestershire sauce, simmer 15 to 20 minutes. Add bean mixture with beef, stir and simmer 15 minutes. Before serving, place cheese slices over top and cover to allow cheese to melt.

Catsup will flow out of the bottle evenly if you just insert a plastic straw; push it to the bottom then remove.

Acine de Pepe Salad

Laurie Dyer
Vancouver, WA

This is my very favorite salad because the pasta is so fun and different! My mother always made this salad when we had a crowd at our home or were expecting company. I have carried on the tradition because it is such an easy salad and can be prepared ahead of time. It makes a large quantity and is yummy (and different than anything people have ever tasted)!

1 box acine de pepe pasta
3 c. mandarin oranges
2 c. pineapple tidbits
1 can crushed pineapple

2 c. marshmallows
1 large container whipped
   topping

Cook pasta according to package instructions and rinse with cool water. Set aside while preparing dressing.

Dressing:

1-3/4 c. pineapple juice
1 c. sugar
2 T. flour

2 egg yolks
1/4 c. lemon juice

Boil pineapple juice and sugar. Add flour and egg yolks, one at a time, stirring for 3 minutes until thick. Add lemon juice. Combine with pasta and allow to marinate overnight. Before serving add oranges, pineapple, marshmallows and whipped topping. Stir well.

Sunday Roast Beef Dinner

Denise Jabaly
Daytona Beach, FL

*My favorite because my husband and kids love it
and it's so easy!*

4 baking potatoes
4 lbs. eye of round roast

garlic salt
garlic cloves

Preheat oven to 500 degrees. Pierce potatoes and place in oven. Generously sprinkle roast with garlic salt. Pierce beef and insert halved or quartered garlic cloves. Place beef in roasting pan, fatty side up. Roast 5 minutes per pound at 500 degrees; high temperature will keep the juices in and give the roast a great flavor. Turn oven off and don't open door. Leave roast in oven for another 25 to 30 minutes. Let roast sit 5 minutes before slicing, then spoon juices over each slice. Serves 4.

*Make a pretty summer centerpiece by filling a watering can with
greenery and a big red gingham bow.*

Homemade Chicken & Noodles

Donna K. Dye
Ray, OH

This is a recipe handed down from my mother. The ingredients are very simple, but they produce a thick, rich broth that tastes wonderful. They're a great side dish for turkey, stuffed pork chops or roast chicken. The secret ingredient is the vinegar; it keeps the noodles tender.

whole chicken
3 c. flour
1 t. salt
5 large eggs

1/2 t. yellow food coloring
white vinegar
chicken broth

Rinse chicken well and place in a 4-quart saucepan. Add enough water to cover and cook until done, approximately one hour. Reserving broth, remove chicken from saucepan, cool and remove from bone. Set aside. In a large mixing bowl, thoroughly combine flour and salt. In a separate mixing bowl, whisk eggs and food coloring togther. Pour enough vinegar in 1/2 of a broken egg shell to fill it, add to egg mixture, whisk again. Make a well in the center of the flour mixture and add egg mixture. Work dough with hands until all ingredients are completely mixed. On a lightly-floured surface work dough until smooth, adding more flour if dough is sticky. Let dough rest 20 minutes; divide dough in half. On a lightly floured surface, roll one section of dough into a circle. Continue to roll dough until thin, noodles will plump up when cooked. Cut circle into quarters, layer quarters on top of one another, flouring well between layers. Cut noodles into three long strips, then cut each of the three strips crossways to desired width; toss with flour to sepa-rate noodles. Set noodles aside and repeat with second portion of dough. Loosely cover with paper toweling and let dry one to 2 hours, or overnight. Bring reserved broth to a boil, adding additional canned broth if necessary to equal approximately 2 quarts. Drop noodles in, a handful at a time, stirring constantly. Reduce heat to a simmer and cook covered for 20 minutes stir-ring occasionally to prevent sticking. Uncover, add reserved chicken, and cook uncovered for another 20 minutes or until noodles are tender. Continue to stir to prevent sticking.

Darn Good Sweet & Sour Pork

Sandy Benham
Sanborn, NY

A favorite because it's so easy to make and nice for guests.

1-1/2 lb. lean shoulder pork, cut into 2-inch strips
2 T. oil
1/2 c. water
2 T. cornstarch
1/2 t. salt
1/4 c. brown sugar
1/4 c. vinegar
1 c. pineapple juice
1/4 c. onion, thinly sliced
1/2 c. green pepper, cut into strips
1 T. soy sauce
1 can pineapple chunks

Brown meat in hot oil, add water, cover and simmer for 45 minutes. Combine cornstarch, salt, brown sugar, vinegar, pineapple juice and soy sauce in saucepan. Cook over medium heat until slightly thick, stirring constantly. Pour sauce over hot pork, let stand 10 minutes, add remaining ingredients and cook an additional 3 minutes.

*Tuck a rocking chair in a corner of your kitchen for
a cozy spot to relax in.*

Tomato Gravy

Lucia Nicol
Marysville, OH

An old favorite great on mashed potatoes. I've never used exact measurements. It tastes better that way!

shortening
flour

canned tomatoes
brown sugar

In a skillet, add a small amount of shortening and flour. Add canned tomatoes, either juice or chunks, enough to make the consistency of gravy. Cook until heated through, add a little brown sugar.

Happiness grows at our own firesides...

-Douglas Terrold

Pile High Surprise

Liz Kenneweg
Gooseberry Patch

When I was a little girl, I recall a cold winter's night when the wind was howling outside and the snow was piling up on the windowpanes. The light that came from a hurricane lamp gave off a golden glow in the kitchen where Mom was busy making mashed potatoes for this recipe. Times have changed, but not my memories.

10 hot dogs	5 strips bacon
3 cups mashed potatoes	1 small onion, sliced in rings
5 slices your favorite type cheese	

Slice hot dogs, 2 per person, lengthwise and lay flat in a casserole dish. Spoon approximately 1/2 cup of mashed potatoes on each serving of hot dogs. Layer with cheese, bacon and onion. Broil for 10 minutes. Serves 5.

Make and store casseroles ahead for quick, easy meals! Simply line a casserole dish with foil, fill with your favorite casserole, then freeze. Once the ingredients are completely frozen, lift the foil and casserole from the dish, wrap tightly in freezer wrap and return to the freezer. When you need a quick meal, pop the frozen casserole back in a dish and bake!

Out-Of-This-World Rolls

Linda L. Murdock
Selah, WA

My favorite recipe because after I began using this recipe I had perfect rolls every time. My husband no longer says, "I wish you could make rolls like Mom's." Now I do!

2 T. yeast	3 eggs, beaten
1/2 c. sugar	5 c. flour
1-1/2 c. warm water	2 t. salt
1/2 c. shortening	butter, melted

Dissolve yeast and 1/2 teaspoon sugar in 1/2 cup warm water; set aside. In a mixing bowl cream shortening and remaining sugar. Add eggs, remaining water and yeast mixture. Beat with an electric mixer or a heavy-duty whisk. Sift flour and salt together, and add to yeast mixture in three batches. Continue beating until glossy in texture. Dough will be sticky, do not add additional flour. Cover bowl and sit in a warm place, let rise one hour. Mix down with hands and cover bowl with a plastic bag that has been oiled inside. Secure bag around bowl with a rubber band to close tightly. Cool overnight in the refrigerator. Dough will continue to rise, make sure bowl is large enough to allow for growth of dough. Remove from refrigerator 2 hours before ready to bake and shape into rolls. Dip rolled dough in melted butter and place in a baking pan, rolls touching. Bake at 350 degrees for 15 to 20 minutes. Makes 3 to 4 dozen rolls.

If you substitute milk for water in your bread recipe, you'll get a finer texture. Water gives bread a coarser texture.

Creamy Frozen Salad

Amy Walker
Tehachapi, CA

This recipe was handed down by my grandmother, it's a real family tradition. Growing up, this special salad was always served at Thanksgiving, Christmas and Easter.

2 c. sour cream
2 T. lemon juice
1/4 c. pecans, chopped
9-oz. can crushed pineapple,
   drained

1/4 c. maraschino cherries,
   sliced
3/4 c. sugar
1/8 t. salt
1 banana, sliced

Combine all ingredients in a mixing bowl using a large spoon. Pour into a one-quart jello mold, paper muffin cups, or muffin tins and freeze. Before serving, loosen from mold by inverting mold and running under warm water.

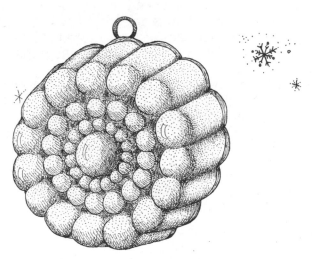

I love everything that is old: old friends, old times, old manners, old books, old wines.

- Oliver Goldsmith

Grandma Lucy's Corn Fritters

Carole Griffin
Mt. Vernon, OH

These fritters remind me of my childhood and the golden days of summer when my grandmother made them.

4 ears sweet corn, cooked
2 eggs, beaten
1/4 c. milk
1/2 c. flour

1 t. baking powder
1 t. sugar
1/2 t. salt
1 T. bacon drippings

In a medium mixing bowl, cut kernels from corn, stir in eggs and milk. Add flour, baking powder, sugar and salt, mix gently. Heat bacon drippings in a skillet on medium high heat. Drop batter from 1/4 cup and cook until delicately browned. Serve with butter and warm maple syrup. Serves 4 to 6.

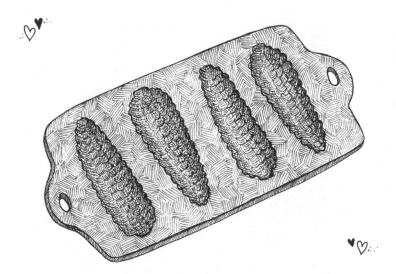

Remove the kernels from ears of corn with a shoe horn! It's easy and just the right size!

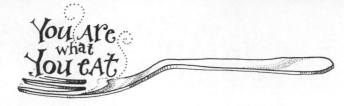

Cottage Potatoes

Delores Hollenbeck
Omaha, NE

*Every time I serve these potatoes someone requests the recipe!
I first had it at my mother-in-law's home and needless to say, I
asked for a copy of it!*

8 to 10 potatoes, boiled until
   tender
1/2 lb. cubed processed
   cheese
1 green pepper, diced
1 small jar pimento, diced

1 medium onion, diced
2 T. parsley, chopped
1 stick margarine
1/2 c. milk
1 slice bread, torn
salt and pepper

Peel and slice potatoes into chunks, mix with cheese, green
pepper, pimento and onion. Combine remaining ingredients and
add to potato mixture. Place in a greased casserole dish and
bake at 350 degrees for 45 to 50 minutes.

A few drops of lemon juice in the water will whiten boiled potatoes.

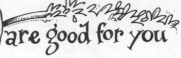
Calico Beans

Cynthia Rogers
Upton, MA

This recipe is perfect for summer barbecues, it serves a crowd!
I serve it in a slow-cooker and let guests help themselves.
Many have a second helping and everyone asks for the recipe.
It's much tastier than any baked bean dish you've tasted!

1/2 lb. ground beef
1/2 lb. bacon
1 c. onion, chopped
1 clove garlic, minced
1/2 c. ketchup
1 t. salt
1/4 c. brown sugar
1 t. dry mustard

2 t. vinegar
16-oz. can lima beans,
   drained
2 16-oz. cans kidney beans,
   drained
3 16-oz. cans baked beans
   in sauce

Brown ground beef, bacon, onion and garlic; drain. Mix and combine with remaining ingredients and bake, covered, at 350 degrees for 45 minutes, or use a slow-cooker set on high for 3 to 4 hours.

Be spontaneous! Gather the family together and go on a picnic to celebrate the beginning of summer and the return of lazy weekends spent in the country.

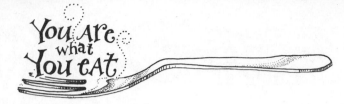

Tangy Glazed Carrots

Teri Lindquist
Gurnee, IL

A different way to serve carrots, children especially love them!

1 lb. carrots, cooked and
   drained
3 T. butter, melted

2 T. brown sugar
1 T. Dijon mustard
1/2 t. ground ginger

Place carrots in a bowl, set aside. Whisk together remaining ingredients and pour over carrots. Toss gently. Makes 6 servings.

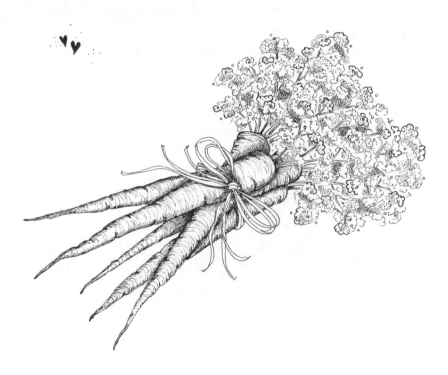

Cooking vegetables ahead of schedule can save time, but they will lose about 1/4 of their vitamin C after a day's refrigeration.

Zucchini "Crab Cakes"

Shirley B. Bowles
Wyoming, DE

Anyone who has ever grown zucchini knows how prolific it can be! One year I gave everyone I know 3 or 4 zucchini and a copy of this recipe. Long after the zucchini were gone I still had people asking me for more! I have a granddaughter who won't eat vegetables, but will eat at least six "crab cakes"! Try and see for yourself!

2 c. zucchini, peeled and
    grated
1 c. seasoned Italian bread
    crumbs

1 T. mayonnaise
1 T. seafood seasoning
2 eggs
1 t. Worcestershire sauce

Combine all ingredients together and pat into cakes. Fry in an oiled skillet or deep fryer. Serves 4 to 6.

You can make bread crumbs with seasoned flavor by whirling your favorite stuffing mix in a blender or food processor.

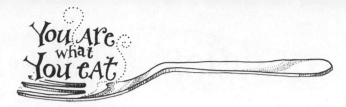

Cheesy Red Potatoes

Mary Ann Nemecek
Springfield, IL

A great dish for holidays, picnics or birthdays...whenever there's a crowd!

5 lbs. red potatoes	1 pt. half-and-half
1 stick butter	1 lb. processed cheese

Cook potatoes in skins the day before serving. Refrigerate overnight, then peel and grate into a 13"x9" pan; set aside. Combine butter, half-and-half and cheese in a saucepan until cheese is melted, let stand at room temperature for one hour. Bake at 375 degrees for one hour or until cheese is golden. Serves 12 to 16.

 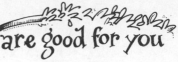
Iowa Scalloped Corn

Karen Klaas
Santa Clara, CA

This corn recipe is flavorful and fluffy in the middle, buttery and crunchy on the outside! My mother and I have made it for years and folks scrape every crumb from the casserole dish!

3 eggs
1 c. milk
2 15-oz. cans cream-style
   corn

1 c. cocktail crackers,
   crushed
1/4 t. pepper
4 T. butter

In a large bowl beat eggs with a whisk until whites and yolks are blended. Stir in milk, corn, crackers and pepper. Pour mixture into a greased 2-quart casserole dish, dot with butter. Bake at 350 degrees for one hour. Serves 6.

When boiling corn, add sugar to the water instead of salt. Sugar will sweeten the corn; salt will make it tough.

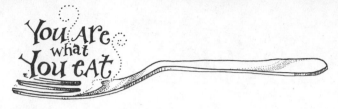

Dad's Favorite Grilled Potatoes

Kim Henry
Library, PA

These potatoes bring back good memories of my father who always enjoyed cooking on the grill. Simple and very tasty!

4 to 5 potatoes	salt and pepper
1 small onion	butter
1 to 2 green peppers	salad seasoning

Slice potatoes, onion and green pepper, sprinkle with salt and pepper to taste. Place in a pan that can be placed on the grill. Add dots of butter, sprinkle with salad seasoning and grill until tender.

A dampened paper towel will remove the silk from an ear of corn if you brush it downward on the cob.

 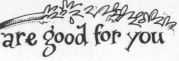

Southern Beans

Lisa Case
Fresno, CA

This recipe was passed down from my Grandma Rainwater. I was raised on this, along with stories about my father's childhood. His father was a pastor and traveled from state to state. Whenever there was a church in need he would go, taking along with his wife and seven children. It's only in looking back on his childhood that my father realizes how poor they were, yet they all felt rich in the things that really mattered. To me this is the ultimate comfort food on a cold day.

1-1/2 lbs. dry pinto beans	1 large onion, chopped
salt to taste	2 or 3 garlic cloves, minced
1 lb. ground beef	1 to 2 c. salsa, optional

Place beans in a stockpot and cover well with water. Boil beans over medium-high heat for 30 minutes. Drain and cover with fresh water. Simmer, stirring occasionally and adding water if necessary. Cook slowly for 4 to 6 hours. Add salt to taste as beans become tender. In a separate skillet, brown ground beef, onion and garlic. Add to beans and continue cooking until beans are tender. Add salsa if desired.

Some have meat who cannot eat,
And some lack meat who want it,
But we have meat and we can eat,
So let the Lord be thanked!
        Old Scottish prayer

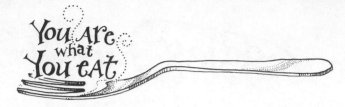

Crunchy Pea Salad

Mary E. Dungan
Gardenville, PA

This salad is beautiful served in a pretty vegetable bowl. Use lots of fresh ingredients for everyone to enjoy!

16-oz. pkg. frozen peas,
   thawed
1 c. celery, chopped
1 can water chestnuts
1/4 c. red onion, chopped
6 slices bacon, fried and
   crumbled

1-1/2 c. mayonnaise-type
   salad dressing
1/4 c. Italian dressing
lettuce leaves
1 c. peanuts

Combine ingredients with dressings, mixing until blended. Line serving dish with lettuce, add peanuts to salad mixture, and spoon into dish. Enough for 8 generous servings.

To keep celery crisp, stand it in a pitcher or crock of cold, salted water and refrigerate it.

Cheesy Oven Fries

Betty Lou Wright
Goodlettsville, TN

These are hard to beat; great tasting!

3 medium baking potatoes
1/3 c. Parmesan cheese
3/4 t. salt

3/4 t. garlic powder
3/4 t. paprika
3 T. margarine, melted

Wash potatoes and cut into wedges or slice into rounds. Combine cheese, salt, garlic powder and paprika and stir well. Arrange potato wedges or rounds on lightly greased 15"x10"x1" pan. Brush margarine on potatoes and sprinkle cheese mixture on top. Bake at 375 degrees, uncovered, for 40 minutes or until potatoes are tender and brown. Makes 3 to 5 servings.

If you let raw potatoes sit in a bowl of cold water for half an hour they'll be crisper when you make home fries or French fries.

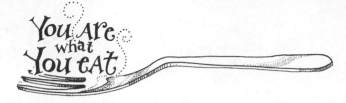

Mimi's Potato Salad

Deidré Rummel Barnett
Louisville, KY

This potato salad is so easy to make. I remember it because my mother's "secret" recipe is the Italian dressing! She and my grandmother would make a huge bowl of it for my five brothers and sisters for every summer gathering while we were growing up. As each child gets married, we receive a huge "potato salad" bowl from my mother!

3 lbs. potatoes
1/2 c. Italian salad dressing
1 stalk celery, chopped
1 green onion, chopped
1/2 c. mayonnaise

salt and pepper to taste
2 radishes, sliced
1 hard-boiled egg, sliced
paprika
parsley sprigs

Rinse potatoes and cook, unpeeled, in boiling water until fork-tender. Drain potatoes and while still warm, carefully peel. Cut in cubes and place in a large bowl. Pour Italian dressing over warm potatoes and gently stir to coat. Let potatoes sit to absorb dressing. Add celery, green onion, mayonnaise and salt and pepper to potatoes. Arrange radish slices on top of potato mixture, and sliced egg on top of radishes. Sprinkle paprika over salad and add parsley around edge. Serve chilled, serves 8 to 10.

Perogees

Mary Plank
Silverton, OR

This is a favorite recipe because it has always been a part of my family. It came from the "old country" in what is now part of Poland. My grandparents fled the country during a time of war, going first to Canada and later moving to the United States. This recipe brings back wonderful memories of family gatherings filled with love and laughter.

6 potatoes, grated	1 egg
dash of salt, pepper and sugar	8 small green onions, chopped
1 pt. cottage cheese	sour cream for garnish

Combine potatoes with salt, pepper and sugar; set aside. In a mixing bowl combine remaining ingredients for filling. Heat enough oil in an iron skillet to cover the bottom and place a spoonful of the potato mixture in, spreading out slightly. Top with a spoonful of filling and cover with enough potato mixture to cover filling. Fry until browned, turn and continue until done. Serve with sour cream if desired.

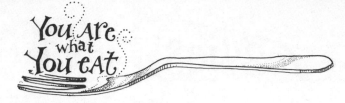

Tomato-Seafood Salad

Alicia Bates
Kent, OH

This is a recipe from my aunt Mary McFerron who is an excellent cook. We usually double this recipe as it disappears fast! There are never any leftovers! Even people who don't care for pasta salad like this salad. It's a great dish for potluck suppers or a cookout!

1/2 c. mayonnaise-type
    salad dressing
1/4 c. Italian salad dressing
2 T. Parmesan, grated
1-1/2 c. chopped crab meat
2 c. tri-colored corkscrew
    pasta, cooked and drained

1 c. broccoli flowerets,
    blanched
1/2 c. green pepper, chopped
1/2 c. tomato, chopped
1/4 c. red onion, minced

Combine salad dressings and cheese, mixing well. Add remaining ingredients and chill.

Thaw your frozen fish in milk. It gets rid of any frozen taste and helps provide a fresh-caught flavor!

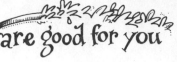

Chuck Wagon Carrots

Sandy Peterson
Glen Ellyn, IL

My favorite recipe because it's the only cooked carrots my family will eat!

3 c. sliced carrots
1/4 c. bacon, cooked and
   crumbled
3 T. butter
1 T. brown sugar, firmly
   packed

2 T. green onions, sliced
1/4 t. salt
1/8 t. pepper

Boil carrots in a 2-quart saucepan until tender, 8 to 12 minutes, drain. Return to pan and add remaining ingredients. Cover and cook over medium heat until heated through.

For a juicier hamburger add 1/2 cup cold water to each pound of beef before you grill it.

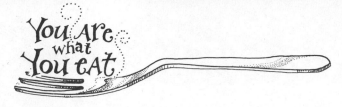

Delightfully Cheesy Potatoes

Blanche T. Yonk
Petersboro, UT

My husband perfected this recipe while he was chairman of our church dinners. He wanted to serve something different and after many tries and much experimenting he came up with this three cheese potato dish. Since then it's become a family favorite. We always called them "Merlin's Cheesy Au Gratin Creamy Potatoes" until someone called them delightfully cheesy and the name stuck! They are a hit anytime, anyplace! Terrific served with baked ham!

8 to 9 medium potatoes	4 c. milk
8 T. butter	8-oz. jar cheese spread
8 T. flour	Parmesan cheese
1 t. salt	1-1/2 c. Cheddar, shredded
1/2 t. pepper	

Cook potatoes in jackets until tender. Cool, peel and cube. Place in a large bowl. Melt butter over low heat in a heavy saucepan. Blend in flour and seasonings. Continue to cook over low heat until mixture is bubbly. Remove from heat and stir in milk. Return to heat and bring to a boil, stirring constantly. Boil for one minute and remove from heat. Stir in cheese spread, and one cup of cheese, stir until cheeses melt. Transfer potatoes to a casserole dish and pour cheese mixture over potatoes, gently stir. Sprinkle generously with Parmesan and remaining Cheddar. Cover and bake at 350 degrees for one hour or until bubbly and slightly brown.

Only two things in this world are too serious to be jested on...
potatoes and marriage.

-American Charity Cookbooks, 1870-1950

Spicy Corn

Lori Mulhern
Rosemount, MN

 A new way to add zip to corn!

1/2 c. creamy buttermilk
  dressing
2 T. parsley
1/4 t. pepper
dash red pepper
2 c. fresh corn, or cooked
  frozen corn

1/2 c. Monterey Jack cheese,
  shredded
1/4 c. green pepper, chopped
1/4 c. green onion, chopped
1/4 c. cucumber, chopped

Combine buttermilk dressing, parsley, pepper and red pepper.
Pour over remaining ingredients, mix well and chill before
serving. Serves 6.

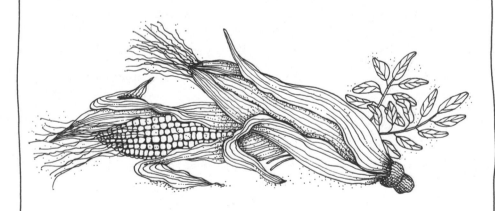

Sprinkle dried herbs such as tarragon, rosemary, oregano, or sage
over your hot coals before grilling; they'll enhance the flavor
of the food.

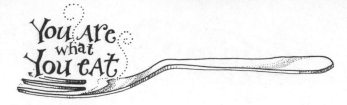

Artichoke Pasta Salad

Lori Davey
Owosso, MI

So easy for a potluck or family gathering!

12 oz. bow tie pasta
6 oz. pitted ripe olives
8-oz. can artichoke hearts,
    chopped

8 oz. feta cheese, cubed
8 oz. mozzarella cheese,
    cubed

Cook pasta according to package directions. Drain, cool and combine with remaining salad ingredients.

Dressing:

1 clove garlic, chopped
1/4 c. basil
1/2 t. dried thyme
1/4 c. Parmesan cheese
3/4 c. olive oil

1/4 c. red wine vinegar
1/4 c. balsamic vinegar
1/4 t. salt
1/8 t. pepper

Place dressing ingredients in a blender and blend well. Gently toss salad mixture with salad dressing and chill. Serves 8 to 10.

Potato Boats

Robyn Fiedler
Tacoma, WA

Similar to twice-baked potatoes, but without all the fat! The squash gives them a different flavor…a great way to serve potatoes.

2 large russett potatoes	1/4 t. cumin
1 lb. butternut squash	1 t. salt
1/4 c. plus 2 t. butter, melted	paprika

Bake potatoes at 425 degrees for 60 minutes. Remove skin from squash, cut squash into cubes and steam 15 minutes. Cut potatoes in half, scoop pulp out and combine with squash, 1/4 cup butter, cumin and salt; mash. Heap into potato shells and brush with remaining butter, sprinkle with paprika. Broil for 5 to 10 minutes.

Is someone special celebrating an anniversary? Create a memory wreath from reminders of that cherished day. Spray paint a heart-shaped grapevine wreath with silver paint. When dry, arrange and glue on pieces of lace, a strand of pearls, ribbon, copies of wedding photos, a silver hair comb, or white gloves. Tuck in baby's breath and dried roses around the keepsakes.

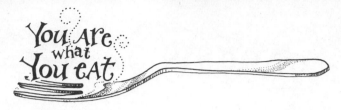
Mom's Red Cabbage

Lisa Rubach
Elkhorn, WI

This is my favorite recipe because of its great aroma while cooking. I remember we could always count on it being on the table for holiday meals. Sometimes my mother would surprise us and make it for Sunday dinner, that was really special!

10 slices bacon, diced
1 medium onion, diced
1 medium head red cabbage, shredded
1 bay leaf
1/2 c. sugar

1/3 c. vinegar
1 t. chicken boullion
1 c. applesauce
1 c. jellied cranberry sauce
2 apples, peeled and sliced

Sauté bacon and onion together in a large skillet. When translucent, add cabbage, bay leaf, sugar, vinegar and chicken boullion. Cook 20 minutes, add applesauce and cranberry sauce. Mix well and simmer 5 minutes. Add apples, mix and serve.

veggies are good for you

Potato Kugel

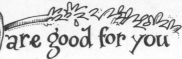

Pat Woods
Syracuse, NY

I remember this recipe because my mother used to make it for my two twin sisters, my brother and me when we were children in the 1950's. She used to make it Friday night with supper, and we could never get enough of it.

6 potatoes, peeled and grated   1/4 c. flour
1 egg   1/2 c. shortening
1/2 c. onion, grated

Mix together all ingredients except shortening and set aside. Heat shortening in a skillet and add mixture. Bake for 15 minutes at 400 degrees, reduce heat to 350 and bake for 1-1/2 hours or until brown. Cut in wedges, serves 6.

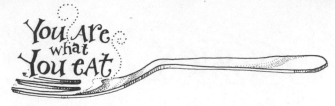

Auntie Carol's Corny Corn Casserole
Sue Young
Crystal Lake, IL

Whenever I make this dish it's a recipe everyone loves, there are never any leftovers and no one leaves until they get the recipe!

1 c. cream-style corn
1 c. corn
1 T. sugar
1 c. sour cream

2 eggs
1 small pkg. cornbread mix
2 sticks butter, melted

Mix all ingredients together and bake in a buttered 9"x9"x2" baking dish at 350 degrees for one hour. Serves 4 to 6.

 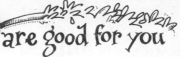
Kanechins

Brandy Riess
New Hope, PA

Kanechins are my favorite recipe because whenever I make them I am able to remember many of the special times I had with my grandmother. She would always make these for me when the weather was cold. This meal was great to warm up with!

1 lb. longhorn Cheddar cheese	flour as needed
4 medium potatoes	1/2 to 1 lb. bacon
1 small onion	1 egg

In a large bowl cut cheese into chunks, set aside. Finely grate potatoes and onion. Add flour to mixture until it forms a thick paste. Fry bacon until crisp and break into small pieces; reserve bacon drippings. Fill a large 6 to 8 quart stockpot with water and bring to a boil. Slowly place small quarter-size amounts of potato mixture into water. When dumplings raise to the top, remove and drain. Place dumplings into the bowl of cheese and mix well. Add bacon, small amount of bacon drippings and egg, mixing well. The hot mixture will safely cook the egg, just salt and pepper to taste. Serve with sour cream or applesauce.

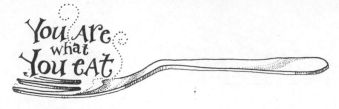

Boston Baked Beans

Kathy Z. Horine
Louisville, KY

Fast to prepare while grilling outdoors.

2 T. brown sugar
2 T. molasses
1/4 c. hot water

3/4 c. catsup
2 16-oz. cans pork and
   beans

Dissolve brown sugar and molasses in hot water. Add catsup and stir. Mix in pork and beans and pour into a 1-1/2 quart baking dish. Microwave 18 minutes on high, or bake uncovered at 350 degrees for one hour. Makes 6 servings.

 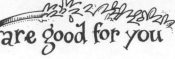

Pea & Shrimp Salad

Judy Voster
Neenah, WI

This is my favorite recipe because my mom always made it for our "feast" celebrations. In the 1950's shrimp was for company or special occasions only. I still think of it as a special salad, but I make it for any occasion too!

15-oz. can early peas, drained
6-1/2 oz. can tiny shrimp, rinsed and drained

1 stalk celery, chopped
2 or 3 T. mayonnaise
1/4 t. salt

Mix all ingredients in a casserole dish, serve chilled. Great served with chicken!

Get up early in the morning and enjoy the rows of just-picked produce from your local farmers' market.

Sweets for the Sweet

Save room for dessert ♥ Save r

Grandma's Molasses Cake

Sonia Schork
Lakeside, AZ

This recipe has been passed down in our family for generations beginning in England in the early 1800's. It's simple and delicious! It was always on our table or in our pantry, served for breakfast, lunch, dinner or snacks with coffee, tea, or milk.

1-1/2 c. all-purpose flour
1/2 c. minus 1 T. shortening
1/2 c. molasses
1/2 c. sugar
1 t. cinnamon
1/2 t. cloves

1/2 c. seeded raisins
1/2 c. pecans, chopped
1-1/2 t. baking soda
1/8 t. salt
1 c. hot water

Preheat oven to 350 degrees and oil an 8-inch cake pan. Combine all ingredients, except hot water, mixing well. Add hot water, batter will be thin. Blend well and pour into prepared pan. Bake 35 minutes.

Roll out leftover pie crust and cut into fun shapes with mini cookie cutters. Bake the cut-outs and spread with jam as a treat for the baker and little "assistants"!

Moravian Sugar Cake

Kathy Martin
Richlandtown, PA

This recipe brings back many sweet memories of my childhood years growing up in Bethlehem, Pennsylvania, a lovely city rich in Moravian traditions. My mother has been making this recipe for many years, and I can still remember the wonderful aroma. She has a magic touch with this!

2 pkgs. yeast
1 c. warm water
1 c. sugar
1/2 t. salt
2 eggs, beaten

1-1/2 c. butter, melted
1 c. mashed potatoes
5 to 6 cups sifted,
    unbleached flour

Soften yeast in water and 2 teaspoons sugar. Allow to stand 5 to 10 minutes. Combine remaining sugar, salt, eggs and one cup melted butter. Gradually beat in mashed potatoes and one cup flour, beat until smooth. Stir in yeast mixture and beat in enough flour to form a soft dough. Cover with a cloth and let rise in a warm place until double in size. Divide dough into 3 portions and press into 3 greased 9 inch square pans. Cover and allow to rise again until double in size. Make indentations 1-inch apart in the dough and spoon in topping.

Topping:

1-1/2 c. light brown sugar

3 t. cinnamon

Blend ingredients and spoon into indentations made in dough. Drizzle remaining 1/2 cup melted butter on top and bake at 350 degrees for 20 minutes.

Concord Grape Pie

Debby Horton
Cincinnati, OH

The Concord grapes we used in this recipe are grown and picked by my family. The original grapes were grown on my great-uncle's farm in Kentucky. He had rows upon rows of grape vines crawling along the fences. In the fall we would pick the grapes and prepare them for the holidays...jelly and jam, pies and wine. Today the tradition continues from the grapes grown in my father's yard. He was able to transplant the love of these grapes from my uncle's farm to his backyard. This family favorite will always be an important ingredient to our holiday gatherings.

1-1/2 lbs. (4 cups) Concord grapes	1/4 t. salt
1 c. sugar	1 T. lemon juice
1/3 c. all-purpose flour	2 T. butter, melted
	9-inch unbaked pastry shell

Slip skins from grapes; set aside. Cover grapes with water and bring to a boil, then reduce heat. Simmer uncovered for 5 minutes then run through a sieve to remove seeds. Combine with skins and add sugar, salt, lemon juice and butter. Pour into pastry shell and bake at 400 degrees for 25 minutes. Sprinkle with topping.

Topping:

1/2 c. flour	1/4 c. butter
1/2 c. sugar	

Sift flour and sugar, cut in butter until crumbly. Sprinkle on top of pie and bake for an additional 15 minutes. Serves 8.

Pie crust is easier to make if all the ingredients are cool.

Favorite Pie Crust

Karen Antonides
Gahanna, OH

My mom and I use this recipe whenever we make a pie, it's been a favorite for over 20 years and we always get excellent results! Whenever either of us make a pie we always ask each other, "Did you use the crust recipe with the vinegar in it?"

4 c. flour	1 T. vinegar
1-3/4 c. shortening	1 egg
1 T. sugar	1/2 c. water
2 t. salt	

With a fork, mix together flour, shortening, sugar and salt. In a separate dish, beat remaining ingredients. Combine both mixtures with a fork until all ingredients are moist. Using hands, mold dough into a ball and chill at least 15 minutes before rolling it into desired shape. Dough can be left in the refrigerator for up to 3 days or it can be frozen until ready to use. Makes 2, 9-inch double pie crusts and a 9-inch shell.

To chill pie crust in a hurry fill a large zipping plastic bag with ice and add one cup of water. Close the bag and place on top of rolled out dough. Within 5 minutes the dough will be thoroughly chilled.

Mom's Apple Dumplings

Sharon Gibbons
Knoxville, TN

These apple dumplings always remind me of growing up and the happiness of home.

6 medium apples
1-1/2 c. sugar
1-1/2 c. water
1/4 t. ground cinnamon
1/4 t. ground nutmeg
8 drops red food coloring

3 T. butter
2 C. flour
2 t. baking powder
1 t. salt
2/3 c. shortening
1/2 c. milk

Peel and core apples. Prepare syrup by mixing sugar, water, cinnamon, nutmeg and food coloring in a saucepan and bring to a boil. Remove from heat and add butter. Set aside. Sift dry ingredients, mix in shortening; add milk and stir until flour is moistened. Roll on a lightly floured surface until approximately 18"x12". Cut into six 6-inch squares and place an apple on each square. Sprinkle generously with additional sugar, nutmeg and cinnamon; dot with butter. Moisten edges of pastry, bring edges to center and pinch together. Place in an ungreased pan and pour syrup over dumplings. Bake for 35 minutes at 375 degrees.

Funnel Cakes

Phyllis M. Peters
Three Rivers, MI

My Mennonite grandmother started a tradition in our family of making funnel cakes, a fascinating skill she had learned from her Amish ancestors. As a child I looked forward to visits to her farmhouse where a simple life attracted me, as well as a loving grandmother who busied herself in the kitchen and welcomed children to assist. All the ingredients to make funnel cakes were placed on a round kitchen table covered with a red and white checked oil cloth. A large kettle of oil heated on the stove until we were ready. We mixed the ingredients and poured the batter in a funnel. As the batter slowly formed a spiral, it sizzled and puffed. What a delight to dust the cakes with powdered sugar! Memories linger. Be creative, start a tradition in your family making funnel cakes. Don't get discouraged, it takes practice, but oh, what fun!

2 eggs, beaten	1 t. baking powder
1/4 c. sugar	1 t. vanilla
1-1/4 c. all-purpose flour	2/3 c. milk
1/4 t. salt	

Combine all ingredients adding enough milk to make a batter. Using a funnel with a 1/2-inch opening, close off the funnel with your finger, fill funnel and controlling the flow with your finger, release batter onto a greased griddle. Use a circular motion, starting in the center, and move outward to make a 3-inch spiral. Cap the flow and start another spiral. Turn cakes once to lightly brown on each side, remove from griddle with a spatula and place on absorbent paper. Sprinkle with a mixture of sugar and cinnamon.

Crow's Nest

Aneda Bryk
Fredericksburg, TX

This recipe's rosy color and crazy name have delighted me since childhood! A four generation recipe, Gramma always picked the rhubarb from her northern garden and made her own cake from scratch. She served it in shallow bowls and passed a small pitcher of light cream around. Now the next generation uses a cake mix and fat-free whipped topping, but the heavenly taste and old-fashioned look are still there!

6 c. rhubarb, coarsely chopped
sugar to taste
margarine

1 box white cake mix
light cream or whipped topping

In a greased and floured 13"x9" pan, place enough chopped rhubarb to make a thick layer in the bottom of the pan. Sprinkle heavily with sugar, to taste. Dot with margarine. Prepare a white cake mix according to the package instructions. Pour cake batter over rhubarb and bake at 350 degrees until cake tests done. Remove pan to a rack to cool. When ready to serve, cut squares and turn each piece fruit side up. Serve on pretty plates and pass a pitcher of light cream or whipped topping.

Mile High Strawberry Pie

Karen Antonides
Gahanna, OH

When our family comes home in the summer, we are welcomed with desserts! My mother-in-law tries to make all the family favorites, which never last long. This is a wonderful, cool summer addition to any gathering. It's easily doubled to serve in a casserole dish.

10 oz. frozen strawberries,
    thawed
1 c. sugar
2 egg whites
1 T. lemon juice
1/8 t. salt

1/2 c. whipping cream
1 t. vanilla
10" baked shell
fresh strawberries, for
    garnish

Combine defrosted strawberries, sugar, egg whites, lemon juice and salt in a large bowl. Beat at medium speed for 15 minutes or until mixture is stiff and holds its shape. Whip the cream, add vanilla and fold into strawberry mixture. Pile lightly into baked shell. Freeze several hours or overnight. Garnish with fresh strawberries if desired. Makes 8 servings.

Pies can be sliced in a snap when you dip the knife in warm water.

Sweets for the Sweet

Raisin Rice Pudding

Carol Jones
Twin Falls, ID

Anytime there was extra milk from the barn this was a good way to use it! During the South Dakota winters when the house was cold, the oven could keep the kitchen warm. Since rice pudding takes a long time to bake, not only did it heat up the kitchen, but the aroma was wonderful!

3 c. milk
1/2 c. raw rice
1/2 t. salt
2/3 c. sugar

raisins
1-1/2 t. vanilla
cinnamon

Place milk, rice, salt, sugar, vanilla and desired amount of raisins in a buttered 1-1/2 quart casserole, sprinkle cinnamon on top. Bake uncovered at 300 degrees for 2 hours. Serve hot or cold.

A late afternoon gathering of good friends is a wonderful way to spend a rainy day.

Madeline Cake

Pat Neaves
Kansas City, MO

This cake brings fond, wonderful and warm memories of my grandmother. If a cook were to have a trademark recipe, this would be hers! She loved this cake and always had one on hand. Caught without one, it was only minutes until we had one, and it was usually gone before it was cool! Yes, the ingredients are right! I have shared this cake with many and always expect a call asking "Where's the salt?", "No baking powder or soda?" No! Just make it! It's wonderful!

3 eggs
1 c. sugar
1 c. flour

1 c. butter
1 t. almond flavoring

Combine eggs, sugar and flour in a mixing bowl. Melt butter and pour over egg mixture. With mixer on low speed, blend ingredients well, add almond flavoring. Continue to beat for 5 minutes. Beating the air in is the only leavening. Spread in a lightly greased 9-inch square pan. Bake at 350 degrees for 25 to 30 minutes. Glaze with a simple almond flavored icing, if desired.

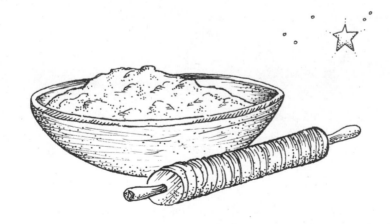

Chocolate Sunday Pie

Sandra Crook
Jacksonville, FL

This pie brings back memories of my grandmother in Alabama. As a child growing up in the south, I enjoyed many wonderful Sunday dinners at my grandmother Dyson's home. Grandmother was cook at the Purefoy Hotel for several decades. Her meals at the hotel and those she prepared for her family were fabulous! Grandmother and the hotel are gone now, but her memory lives on in this delicious chocolate pie.

1-1/2 c. sugar	3 egg yolks
4 T. all-purpose flour	1 T. butter
5 T. cocoa powder	1 t. vanilla
2 c. milk	9-inch prebaked pie shell

In a medium saucepan combine sugar, flour and cocoa. Stir until mixture is well blended. Slowly pour in milk, stirring well. Slightly beat the egg yolks and gradually add to chocolate mixture; add butter. Over medium heat, cook mixture until thick, about 20 minutes, stirring often. When thick, remove from heat and stir in vanilla. Pour into a pre-baked pie shell and top with meringue.

Meringue:

3 egg whites	1/4 c. sugar
1/4 t. cream of tartar	

Beat egg whites and cream of tartar until foamy, gradually add sugar. Continue to beat until stiff peaks form. Spread over pie filling and swirl. Bake at 350 degrees for 10 minutes, or until meringue is golden.

Superfine sugar will make a lighter meringue than granulated sugar. Simply whirl granulated sugar in a food processor for a few minutes until very fine.

Sponge Candy

Cheryl Volbruck
Costa Mesa, CA

At each Christmas holiday I try to introduce at least one new sweet treat for my family and guests to try. I found this sponge candy recipe about a year ago and everyone raved over it; my sister begged for the recipe! I was so happy to share it with her, she couldn't believe how easy it was to make. People will not believe you made this candy!

1 c. dark corn syrup	3 squares chocolate
1 c. sugar	1 c. chocolate chips
1 T. vinegar	1" square paraffin, melted
1 T. baking soda	

Combine corn syrup, sugar and vinegar, bring to the hard-crack stage (290 to 300 degrees on a candy thermometer.) Remove from heat and add baking soda; stir well. Work quickly, mixture foams at this stage, and pour into a buttered 9"x9"x2" pan, do not spread. When cool, slide into a clear plastic bag and break into pieces. Heat chocolate chips and paraffin, carefully dip pieces into topping, place on wax paper until set.

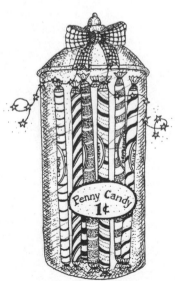

Paint an empty food can in navy, barn red or mustard and tie a homespun bow around the outside, glue a big button in the middle of your bow. Perfect for holding little treats like homemade candy.

Sweet Apple Buckle

Joann Drescher
Utica, NY

Will make your home smell wonderful! It's delicious and easy.

10 apples
1 c. all-purpose flour
1 c. sugar
1 t. baking powder

1/2 t. salt
1 egg
1/2 c. butter, melted
cinnamon

Peel, core and slice apples. Arrange in a 13"x9"x2" baking dish. Combine flour, sugar, baking powder and salt. Using a pastry blender, add egg to mixture and blend until crumbly; sprinkle over apples. Pour butter over topping and sprinkle lightly with cinnamon. Bake at 350 degrees for 45 minutes. Serve with whipped cream if desired.

White Buttermilk Cake

Kristy Boulds
Eldorado, IL

I was raised in a great family. My mom and dad loved to cook and entertain us, our friends and family. My dad would always handle the meat and Mom would handle the rest. When Mom made this cake, even Dad would be like a child waiting to lick the bowl when she made the icing!

3/4 c. butter
2-1/4 c. sugar
3 c. flour
1-1/2 c. buttermilk
1-1/2 t. baking powder

3/4 t. baking soda
3/4 t. salt
4 or 5 egg whites, beaten
1 t. vanilla

Mix butter, 1-1/2 cups sugar, flour, buttermilk, baking powder, baking soda and salt. Beat egg whites with remaining sugar and vanilla; add to mixture. Pour into a prepared cake pan and bake at 350 degrees for one hour. Allow to cool, then ice.

Icing:

2 c. sugar
1/2 c. water
2 T. light corn syrup

2 egg whites, beaten
flaked coconut

Combine sugar, water and corn syrup. Cook over medium heat until mixture reaches a hard boil. While beating egg whites, gradually add hot mixture. Continue beating until mixture loses white glaze appearance. Ice cake and sprinkle with coconut on top.

They had so many puddings, salads, sandwiches and pies, That a feller wisht his stomach was as hungry as his eyes.

—American Charity Cookbooks, 1870-1950

Annie's Bread Pudding

Annie Bateman
Maple Plain, MN

When autumn comes to Minnesota, our family starts longing for a warm fireplace, acorn squash, homemade soups, fresh-baked bread, apple pie and bread pudding. Bread pudding fills the house with a welcome home aroma. It is especially good topped with half-and-half or milk.

1/4 c. butter
3/4 t. ginger
1/2 t. cinnamon
1/4 t. salt
8 slices bread

1/2 c. raisins
4 eggs, beaten
1/4 c. honey
1/4 c. brown sugar
4 c. milk

Cream first four ingredients together until fluffy. Spread each bread slice with butter mixture and layer with raisins in 9"x5"x3" loaf pan. Combine eggs, honey, brown sugar and milk in a large mixing bowl and pour over bread, allow to stand 15 to 20 minutes. Place loaf pan in another baking dish half full with water. Bake at 325 degrees for one hour or until knife inserted in center comes out clean.

Cherries In The Snow

Lynn Peterson
Racine, WI

This recipe stirs up memories just saying the name! My grandma would make this pie on very special occasions when it was requested, and <u>only</u> in the winter. If we asked her why she wouldn't make it in the summer, she would always say, "It makes the winter a special time, besides, whoever heard of snow in the summer?" Luckily for us winters in Wisconsin are long! Because it brings memories of Grandma back so clearly, I too only make this pie in the winter.

3 oz. cream cheese
1/2 c. sugar
1/2 t. vanilla
1/4 t. almond flavoring

1/2 pt. whipping cream
9-inch baked pie shell
20-oz. can cherry pie filling

Cream together cream cheese, sugar, vanilla and almond flavoring. Blend whipping cream to equal one cup. Fold into crcam cheese mixture and pour into pie shell. Top with pie filling, chill 8 hours.

Crustless Pumpkin Pie

Linda Webb
Gooseberry Patch

 A great alternative to pumpkin pie!

4 eggs
16-oz. can pumpkin
2 t. pumpkin pie spice
1 t. salt
1-1/2 c. sugar

12-oz. can evaporated milk
1 box yellow cake mix
1 c. nuts, chopped
2 sticks butter, melted

Combine eggs, pumpkin, spice, salt, sugar and evaporated milk blending well. Pour into an ungreased 13"x9" baking dish and sprinkle cake mix over top. Sprinkle on chopped nuts. Drizzle butter onto cake mix, do not stir. Bake at 350 degrees for 45 minutes to an hour, testing for doneness. Serve with whipped topping if desired.

Homemade Vanilla Pudding

Shannon Barnhart
Ashley, OH

Try this old-fashioned pudding; the real thing!

1/3 c. sugar
1 T. plus 1 t. cornstarch
2 c. milk

3 eggs, lightly beaten
1-1/2 t. vanilla

In a saucepan, combine sugar and cornstarch, whisk in milk. Cook over medium heat until just bubbling; reduce heat to low and simmer one minute. Whisk 1/2 cup of mixture into eggs and gradually add back into milk saucepan. Cook over low heat, stirring constantly until thick enough to coat the back of a spoon. Remove from heat and add vanilla. Pour into a mixing bowl, cover tightly with plastic wrap and chill 30 minutes until set. Makes 6 servings. For variety add cooked rice for instant rice pudding, or substitute dark brown sugar for white sugar, a great butterscotch flavor.

Chocolate leaves are a great dessert garnish! Melt 4 squares of semi-sweet chocolate and brush on the undersides of washed and dried, non-toxic leaves. Place leaves on wax paper-lined cookie sheet and refrigerate 15 minutes, then carefully peel leaves away from chocolate. Refrigerate until ready to use.

Chocolate Cake

Susan Day
Alfred, ME

When I was 12 years old I was going to make a chocolate cake for the first time by myself. My grandmother was coming to visit on this occasion and faithfully, I followed every instruction. It was in the oven only a few minutes when a miserable odor was detected. As my grandmother walked through the door, I pulled the cake from the oven realizing that I had set the oven on broil instead of bake. Without even taking her coat off, Gram went to the stove, took a spatula and scraped the burnt top off the cake. She spoke softly of saving the cake and made my embarrassment disappear as we put it back into the oven to bake. My first cake wasn't quite as good as Gram's and I've made the cake dozens of times since and never made the same mistake, but I will never forget my first time and my grandmother's kindness.

2 c. sugar	1/2 c. cocoa
3/4 c. butter, softened	2 t. baking soda
1-1/2 c. boiling water	2 eggs, beaten
2 c. flour	1 t. vanilla
1/2 t. salt	1 T. lemon juice
1 t. baking powder	

Preheat oven to 350 degrees. Cream sugar and butter in a large bowl, add water and mix well. Combine all dry ingredients thoroughly and add to butter mixture. Add eggs, vanilla and lemon juice, mixing batter well. Pour into a greased 13"x9" pan and bake for 35 minutes.

Someone has said, can you beat it?
You cannot have your cake and eat it!

—American Charity Cookbooks, 1870-1950

Vanilla Ice Cream

Bobbie Jean Morgan
Tulsa, OK

When I was a child, my sister, two brothers and I would go to our grandmother's house in the summer. If it was an especially hot day, she would make ice cream for us. It seemed to take forever because of the steps in preparing it and we must have driven her crazy always wanting to look into the freezer to see if it was finished yet! She was very patient with us and made it for us often.

3 qts. whole milk	1/2 c. flour
6 eggs	1 t. vanilla
2-1/2 c. sugar	1 qt. light cream
1/4 t. salt	

Scald 2 quarts of milk and set aside. Beat eggs, sugar, salt and flour until smooth, gradually add to hot milk. Cook until thick then remove from heat. Add vanilla and remaining milk and cream, stirring until smooth. Cool and pour into pans. Turn refrigerator to coldest setting and let pans cool until mixture is mushy. Remove, beat mixture well and place pans in freezer until firm. Makes one gallon.

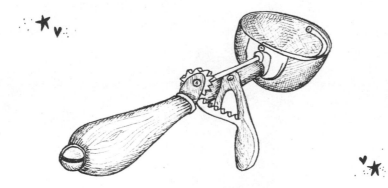

Add fun to dessert! Serve ice cream in foil-lined flower pots and add a cookie-on-a-skewer flower.

Blueberry Pie Dessert

Melissa Maneval
West Unity, OH

This recipe has become a Christmas Eve tradition at my parents' house. We would always open gifts from our grand-parents first and all the excitement and hard work made us hungry, even though we had just finished a huge meal! Sharing this dessert was always a special way to end the evening because we all shared stories and memories. My grandmother has since passed away and now this tradition means even more to me each year.

16 graham crackers, crushed
1/2 c. margarine, melted
1 c. sugar, separated
8-oz. pkg. cream cheese

2 eggs
20-oz. can blueberry pie
    filling
whipped topping for Garnish

Combine crackers with margarine and 1/2 cup sugar. Press into the bottom of a greased 13"x9" baking dish. Beat cream cheese, remaining sugar and eggs. Pour over crust and bake at 350 degrees for 20 minutes. Cool then cover with pie filling. Cut into squares and serve with whipped cream. Serves 15 to 20.

Dutch Apple Crumb Pie

Sammy Polizzi-Morrison
Aurora, CO

My grandmother's recipe for Dutch apple crumb pie is delicious, easy to make and smells wonderful!

5 to 7 tart apples, sliced
9" unbaked pastry shell
1/2 c. sugar
1-1/2 t. cinnamon
1/2 c. brown sugar

3/4 c. flour
1/3 c. butter
whipped cream or ice cream
   for topping

♥

Place apples in pastry shell. Combine sugar and cinnamon and sprinkle over apples. Combine brown sugar and flour, cut in butter until crumbly and sprinkle over apples. Bake at 400 degrees for 40 minutes. Serve with whipped cream or ice cream. Serves 6 to 8.

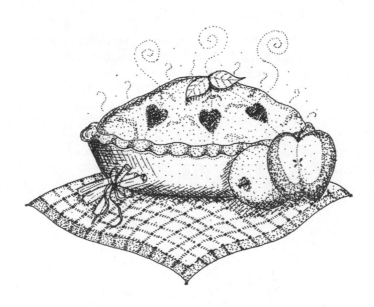

Host an old-fashioned pie party. Invite friends and family to bring their very best pies for sharing and some light-hearted judging!

Old-Fashioned Fudge

Rebecca Chrisman
Citrus Heights, CA

My grandmother always made this fudge for my brothers and me when she would come for a visit. My mother gave me my grandmother's cookbook, which was published in 1930, and so many of the pages are worn and spotted from use over the years. Many recipes my grandmother made were never written down, but she always used her cookbook for this fudge recipe. Over the years I've found it needs to be made exactly as it was written 60 years ago. I tried some modern shortcuts but they didn't work! This fudge brings back wonderful memories of a quieter time with less stress.

2 squares unsweetened chocolate	2 T. light corn syrup
2 c. sugar	1 c. evaporated milk
1/4 t. salt	1 t. vanilla
	3/4 c. nuts

Melt chocolate in a saucepan, add sugar, salt and corn syrup, mixing well. Add milk and blend. Bring ingredients to a boil, cook rapidly until sugar is dissolved, stirring constantly. Turn heat down to a low boil and continue to cook slowly until mixture reaches soft ball stage. Cool without stirring until the hand can be held comfortably on the bottom of the saucepan. Add vanilla and beat vigorously until thick and creamy. Add nuts and pour into a greased 8"x8" square pan. When completely cool, cut into squares.

An easy gift for a new neighbor or friends...wrap candied apples, chocolate-coated pretzels, or fudge in colored cellophane and tie with raffia.

Potato Candy

Julie Messier
Durham, NC

Potato candy was a favorite when I was growing up in Ohio. My mother was raised in an Amish community and prepared this candy every Christmas for her seven children. She hid the 5 pound bag in her closet, and we would sneak in and get several pieces. Come Christmas morning, half of the candy had already been eaten, much to her surprise. Try it; I'm sure you'll like it.

1 lb. unsweetened shredded
   coconut
2 medium potatoes, cooked
   and mashed
1 lb. English walnuts,
   ground

2 lbs. powdered sugar
semi-sweet chocolate chips

Combine coconut, potatoes and walnuts, mixing well; refrigerate several hours. Shape into walnut-sized balls and roll in powdered sugar. Drizzle melted semi-sweet chocolate over candy for a delicious treat.

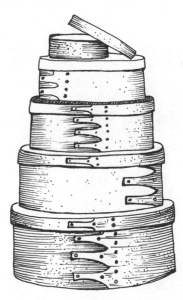

Chocolate Angel Food Cake

Sharon Niemann
Fayette, PA

A special recipe that reminds me of times spent with my mother. While we prepared it, we would talk about how Grandma would make it then put it on the porch to cool.

3/4 c. cake flour
5 T. cocoa
1-1/2 c. sugar
1-3/4 c. egg whites (approximately 12 large eggs)
3/4 t. salt

1-1/2 t. cream of tartar
1 t. vanilla

Sift flour, cocoa and half the sugar, set aside. Beat egg whites with salt until frothy. Add cream of tartar and beat until stiff, but not dry. Add remaining sugar, one tablespoon at a time, folding in thoroughly; add vanilla. Sift flour mixture, and gently fold into egg mixture. Pour into an angel food cake pan and bake at 325 degrees for 75 minutes. Remove from oven and cool cake by inverting cake pan on top of a pop bottle. Makes 16 servings.

Egg whites will have greater volume if you whip them when they're at room temperature.

Snow On A Dirt Road

Joellen Crouch
Lower Lake, CA

My favorite recipe because it reminds me of the first cold, snowy day of the year in my childhood. Mother would have this warm, sweet treat for us after school. It looked like our old road, hence the name!

1/2 c. margarine, softened	1/2 c. coconut
1-1/2 c. brown sugar	1 t. vanilla
1 c. plus 2 T. flour, divided	pinch of salt
2 large eggs	1/2 c. powdered sugar
1 c. pecans, chopped	

Cream margarine, 1/2 cup brown sugar and one cup flour together to form crust. Press in the bottom of an 8-inch square pan. Bake at 350 degrees for 20 minutes. Beat eggs until light and add sugar until thick. Toss pecans, coconut and remaining flour and add to egg mixture. Add vanilla and salt. Pour over hot crust, and bake an additional 20 minutes. Cool and dust heavily with powdered sugar. Makes 16 squares.

Texas Sheet Cake

Tami Bowman
Gooseberry Patch

*This has been my husband's birthday cake every year
since he was little!*

1 c. water	1/2 t. salt
4 T. cocoa	2 eggs
2 sticks butter	1/2 c. sour cream
2 c. flour	1 t. baking soda
2 c. sugar	

Bring water, cocoa and butter to a boil. Remove from heat and add flour, sugar and salt, mixing well. Beat in eggs, sour cream and baking soda and pour into a greased jelly roll pan. Bake at 375 degrees for 20 to 22 minutes. Top with frosting while still hot from the oven.

Frosting:

1 stick butter	1 lb. powdered sugar
4 T. cocoa	1 t. vanilla
6 T. milk	1 c. walnuts, chopped

Combine butter, cocoa and milk and bring to a boil. Remove from heat and stir in remaining ingredients. Beat well and spread over hot cake.

A great gift for your grown child; write out the recipe for their favorite birthday cake and have it framed together with some of their most memorable birthday photos. They'll be delighted!

Tin Can Ice Cream

Christi Miller
New Paris, PA

An unusual recipe, fun and it makes the best ice cream! I don't know where it originated, but we had this at my husband's reunion and everyone loved it. A great project for kids on a summer day!

1 c. milk
1 c. whipping cream
1/2 c. sugar

1/2 t. vanilla
nuts or fruit if desired

Place all ingredients in a one pound coffee can with a tight fitting lid. Additionally secure lid with masking tape. Place coffee can in a larger 3 pound coffee can with a tight fitting lid. Pack crushed ice around the smaller can, sprinkle 3/4 cup rock salt around the top. Secure lid again. Roll back and forth for 10 minutes, check, mix ice cream with spatula, secure lids, roll for 5 more minutes. Add ice as needed.

Mini cookie cutters make excellent chocolate cut-outs. Melt 4 squares of semi-sweet chocolate and pour into a wax paper-lined cookie sheet. With a spatula, spread chocolate to 1/8-inch thickness and refrigerate 15 minutes. Cut shapes with cutters then immediately lift with a spatula and refrigerate until ready to use.

Grandma's Chocolate Pudding
Karen Ferbezar
Shawnee, KS

This recipe holds many fond, warm memories for me because Grandma, who is now 97 years old, made it with love! I remember my grandmother making this for my brothers and me when we were children and she continued to do so when we grew up. If we showed up unexpectedly, she still managed to whip up a batch! When I stayed with her and grandpa for summertime visits, she would let me help her make it, now I make it for my family.

1/2 c. sugar	1 egg
2 heaping T. flour	1-3/4 c. milk
2 T. cocoa	1 t. vanilla
water	1 t. butter

In a mixing bowl combine sugar, flour and cocoa with enough water to make a paste. Mix in egg and beat well. Add milk, stir well and pour into a saucepan. Cook over medium heat until bubbly. Let cool then add vanilla and butter. Serves 4, but has been known to serve only 2!

Layer chocolate pudding in a tall stemmed glass and top with raspberries and a sprig of mint.

Oatmeal Cake

Carolyn Gulley
Cumberland Gap, TN

My favorite recipe, not only because it's delicious, but because of the way we received the recipe. My mom bought an old wooden recipe box at a flea market and inside it she found this recipe written on a folded-up piece of paper. She decided to try it for the first time at Thanksgiving. Everyone loved it and now it's a holiday favorite and tradition!

1-1/2 c. water, boiling
1 c. quick cooking oatmeal
1/2 c. oil
1 c. brown sugar

1 c. sugar
2 eggs
1-1/2 c. self-rising flour
1 t. cinnamon

Pour boiling water over oats, stir and let stand until cool. Combine oil, sugars and egg together; set aside. Sift flour and cinnamon and add to oat and egg mixtures; stir well. Bake in an oiled 12"x9" pan at 350 degrees for 35 to 40 minutes. Ice while still warm.

Icing:

1/2 c. milk
1 c. brown sugar
1 stick butter

1 can coconut
1/2 c. pecans
1 t. vanilla

Combine milk, brown sugar and butter in a saucepan, bring to a boil. Boil for 2 minutes. Remove from heat, add coconut, pecans and vanilla. Spread over cake while still warm in pan. Serves 10 to 12.

For baking it's best to use large eggs. Extra large eggs may cause cakes to fall when they cool.

Sweets for the Sweet

Cherry Delight

Dianna Runyan
Delaware, OH

A wonderful dessert, just forget about the calories!

2 c. graham cracker crumbs
4 T. sugar
4 T. butter, melted
2 8-oz. pkgs. cream cheese, softened

2 eggs. slightly beaten
1 c. sugar
1 t. vanilla
8-oz. can cherry pie filling

Combine graham cracker crumbs, sugar and butter and press into a 13"x9" baking dish. Beat cream cheese, eggs, sugar and vanilla together until fluffy and pour into crust. Bake at 350 degrees for 15 to 20 minutes until set. Cool for 2 hours. When completely cooled, top with pie filling.

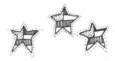

Make chocolate cups to hold strawberries, kiwi, or ice cream. Melt 8 ounces of semi-sweet chocolate and using a pastry brush, spread on the inside of 10 foil baking cups. Set cups in muffin pans and chill for one hour. Carefully peel foil off and refrigerate until serving time.

Nut Rolls

Robin Pavlik Manwiller
Shillington, PA

Nut Rolls remind me of good times spent in the kitchen with my mother and grandmother.

1 yeast cake
1 c. milk, warm
4 T. sugar
5 c. flour
6 eggs, separated and lightly
   beaten

1/2 lb. butter
2 t. salt
2 T. shortening
2 c. milk, scalded
1 t. vanilla

Mix first three ingredients and 2 cups flour; set aside for about 1/2 hour. Combine yolks, butter, salt, shortening and milk stirring until well blended; add to yeast mixture. Beat egg whites until firm, add vanilla and combine with yeast mixture. Mixing well, gradually add in remaining cups of flour and knead until smooth and elastic. Cover with a towel and set aside until double in size. Punch down dough and allow to rise again. Repeat this step twice more. When dough is light, turn out onto a lightly floured board and divide into six parts. Roll out 1/4" thick and spread with nut filling. Bake at 350 degrees for 45minutes.

Nut Filling:

2 lbs. walnuts, ground
2 c. sugar

2 T. butter, melted
4 T. milk

Combine all ingredients and spread on rolled out dough. Roll jelly-roll style and bake. Makes 6 nut rolls.

Angel Food Candy

Louy Danube
Merrimac, WI

One year we made this recipe and it was especially memorable. At our annual Cookie, Candy and Craft Day, all the kids and adults had been creating goodies when my husband rushed into the kitchen to announce that a helicopter had landed in a field across from the house. He and the children drove to the site. They visited with Air National Guardsman who had to land because of technical problems. We brought them a "Care Package" of our newly created goodies as they awaited rescue. They in turn let everyone who wanted to, sit in the cockpit and play with the instrument panels. The two Guardsmen gave the kids an assortment of their food rations as an exchange gift for the homemade candies and cookies we shared. Each year, it seems, some special magic happens as we prepare and pack goodie boxes. It's a great day for sharing Christmas stories and music as we enjoy three generations of companionship.

2 c. brown sugar
2 c. light corn syrup

4 t. baking soda
semi-sweet chocolate, melted

In a 3-quart saucepan combine sugar and corn syrup until candy thermometer reads 300 degrees. Remove saucepan from heat and add baking soda. Stir quickly, as this foams up. Butter sides and bottom of a 13"x9" pan, pour mixture into pan and cool. Break into pieces and dip into melted semi-sweet chocolate.

Give a special delivery package to someone who needs cheering up. Paint an old wooden crate and fill it with an assortment of homemade goodies packed in tins, baskets, bags and jars.

Earthquake Cake

Diane Rogers
Uniontown, OH

A rich and delicious recipe from my mother-in-law!

1 c. pecans, chopped	8 oz. cream cheese
1 c. coconut	1 lb. powdered sugar
German chocolate cake mix	1/4 c. brown sugar
1/2 c. margarine, softened	1 t. vanilla

In a 13"x9" pan, sprinkle pecans and coconut. Prepare cake mix according to package directions; pour over pecans and coconut. Mix remaining ingredients together and drop by spoonfuls on cake mix. Place pan in a 350 degree oven and bake for 50 to 55 minutes. You may want to place a cookie sheet under the cake pan. Let cool and cut into squares.

Combine one cup solid shortening and 1/2 cup flour and store in a plastic container with a tight fitting lid. When you need to grease a cake pan quickly, place your hand in a plastic sandwich bag and scoop out enough of the mixture to apply to your pan. When you're done, toss the plastic bag...so neat and clean!

ᴓSweets for the Sweet

Blackberry Cobbler

Pat Habiger
Spearville, KS

My grandmother made this cobbler when I was a little girl. I would play on Grandpa and Grandma's farm with the large garden, goldfish tank and a tree swing that would almost touch the sky! Grandma would crochet, quilt and make the greatest desserts. Grandpa would work in the fields and the garden and watch us put on plays outside in the yard on summer evenings.

1 c. butter, divided
1 c. plus 2 T. sugar, divided
1 c. water
1-1/2 c. self-rising flour
1/3 c. milk, room
     temperature

2 c. fresh or frozen
     blackberries
1 t. ground cinnamon

In a 10-inch round or oval baking dish, melt 1/2 cup butter; set aside. In a saucepan, heat one cup sugar and water until sugar is dissolved. Place flour in a large mixing bowl and cut in remaining butter until crumbs form. Add milk and stir with a fork to form a dough. Continue stirring until dough leaves the sides of the bowl. Turn out on a floured board; knead three or four times and roll into a 11"x9" rectangle, 1/4-inch thick. Spread berries over dough, sprinkle with cinnamon and roll up, jelly-roll style. Cut into 1/4-inch slices and carefully lay slices in baking dish over butter. Pour sugar syrup around slices. Bake at 350 degrees for 45 minutes. Sprinkle remaining sugar over top and bake 15 minutes more. Serve warm or cold. Makes 8 servings.

Are you making a quilt for yourself or a friend? If so, embroider your signature and the date in one corner. This will identify for future generations the ancestor who spent so many loving hours quilting.

Noodle Kugel

Liz Plotnick
Gooseberry Patch

A traditional family dish served at all family weddings.

1 lb. cottage cheese	1 t. salt
1 c. sour cream	2 t. lemon juice
4 eggs	1 lb. noodles
1 c. sugar	1 c. raisins

Combine all ingredients, except noodles and raisins, in a blender. Whirl until smooth, pour into a large mixing bowl. Cook noodles according to package directions, drain and combine with cottage cheese mixture; blend in raisins. Pour into a 13"x9" casserole dish and bake at 350 degrees for 45 to 50 minutes.

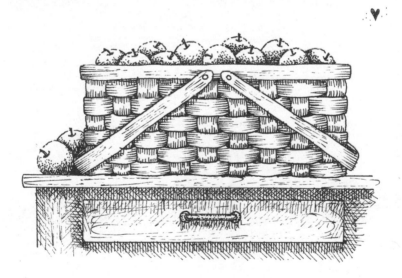

Make your dining table romantic. Tie whispy bows of tulle or satin on the corners of your table. Drape the chairs in netting and tie a lace bow around each chair back.

Index

Index

picture albums the cookie jar Dad's favorite chair tooth under your pillow pictures on the fridge family reunions haven't you grown? sandlot baseball apple-picking egg hunts movies & popcorn scary pumpkins birthdays

picture albums · the cookie jar · Dad's favorite chair · tooth under your pillow · pictures on the fridge · family reunions · haven't you grown? · sandlot baseball · apple-picking · egg hunts · movies & popcorn · scary pumpkins · birthdays

picture albums the cookie jar Dad's favorite chair tooth under your pillow pictures on the fridge family reunions haven't you grown? sandlot baseball apple-picking egg hunts movies & popcorn scary pumpkins birthdays

picture albums the cookie jar Dad's favorite chair tooth under your pillow pictures on the fridge family reunions haven't you grown? sandlot baseball apple-picking egg hunts movies & popcorn scary pumpkins birthdays

picture albums 📖 the cookie jar 🍪 Dad's favorite chair 🦷 tooth under your pillow 🛏 pictures on the fridge 🖼 family reunions 💗 haven't you grown? 🙂 sand lot baseball ⚾ apple-picking 🍎 egg hunts 🥚 movies & popcorn 🍿 scary pumpkins 🎃 birthdays ✳

picture albums 📖 the cookie jar 🍪 Dad's favorite chair 🪑 tooth under your pillow 🗒 pictures on the fridge 🖼 family reunions 🙂 sandlot baseball ⚾ haven't you grown? 😊 apple-picking 🍎 egg hunts 🥚 movies & popcorn 🍿 scary pumpkins 🎃 birthdays 🎂

We've cooked up a whole collection of Gooseberry Patch™ books!

Have a taste for more? Call us toll-free at
1-800-854-6673

We'll send you our latest catalog filled with snowmen, Santas, ornaments, candles, cookie cutters, gourmet goodies, salt-glazed pottery collectibles and MORE...including our best-selling cookbooks!

Phone us:
·800·854·6673

Fax us:
1·740·363·7225

Visit our website:
www.gooseberrypatch.com

Send us your favorite recipe!

and the memory that makes it special for you!* We're putting together a brand new **Gooseberry Patch** cookbook, and you're invited to participate. If we select your recipe, your name will appear right along with it...and you'll receive a FREE copy of the book! Mail to:

Vickie & Jo Ann
Gooseberry Patch, Dept. BOOK
P.O. Box 190
Delaware, Ohio 43015

*Please help us by including the number of servings and all other necessary information!

picture albums 📖 the cookie jar 🍪 Dad's favorite chair 🪑 tooth under your pillow 🛏 pictures on the fridge 📷 family reunions ♡ haven't you grown? ☺ sand lot baseball ⚾ apple-picking 🍎 egg hunts 🥚 movies & popcorn 🎬 scary pumpkins 🎃 birthdays